PICTURE BOOK OF COUNTRY SEASONS

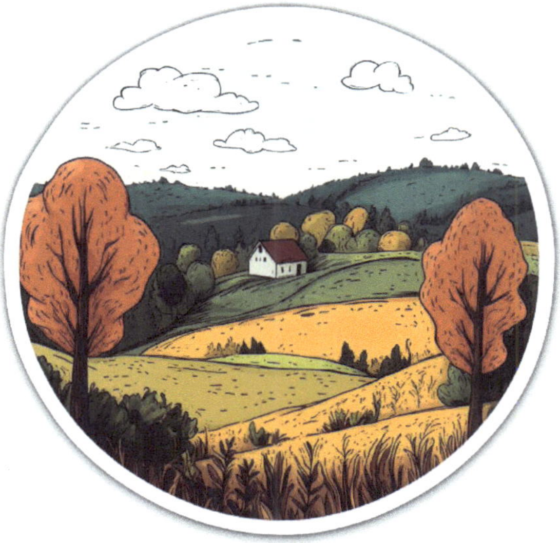

...By...

Ella Caldwell

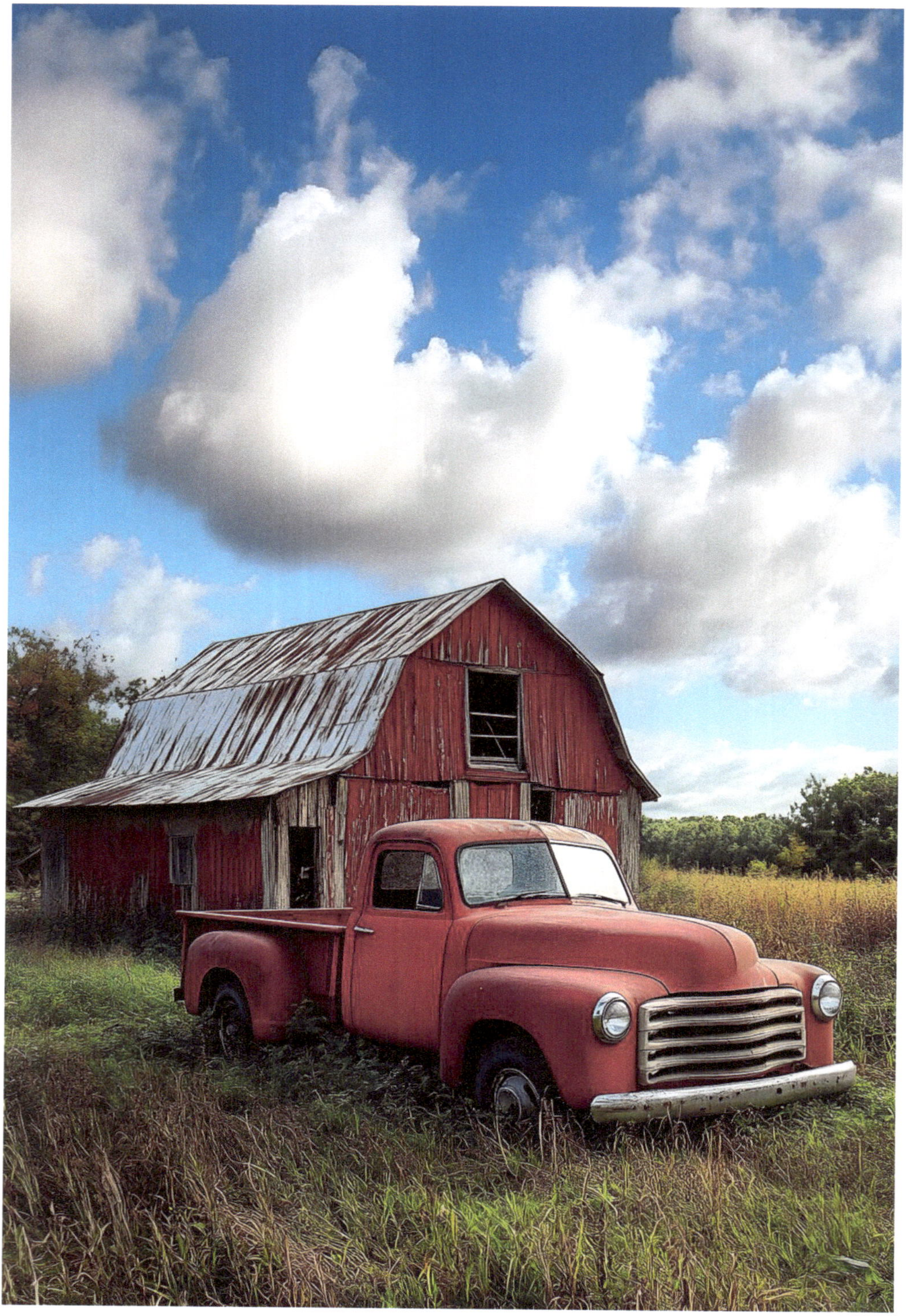

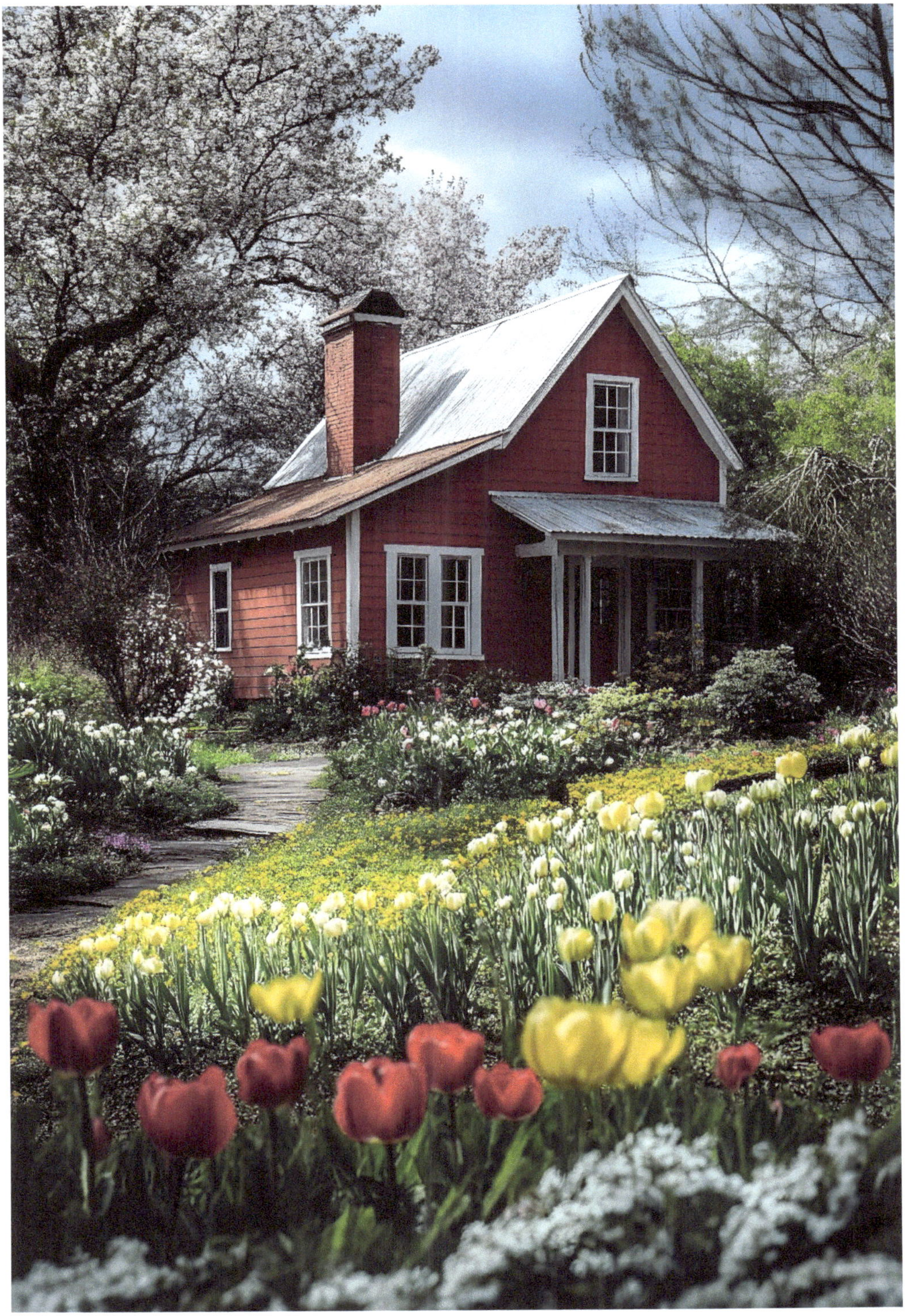

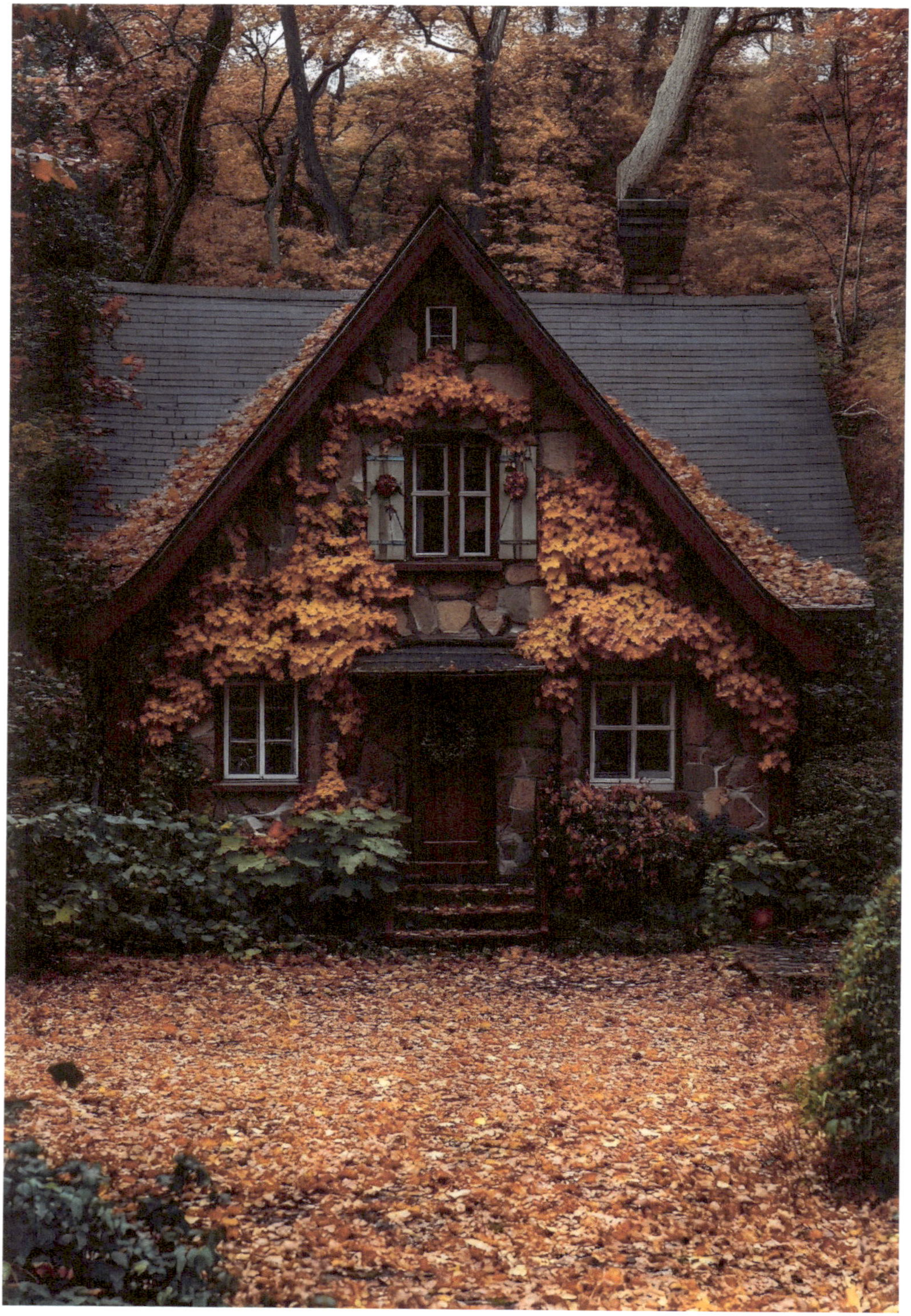

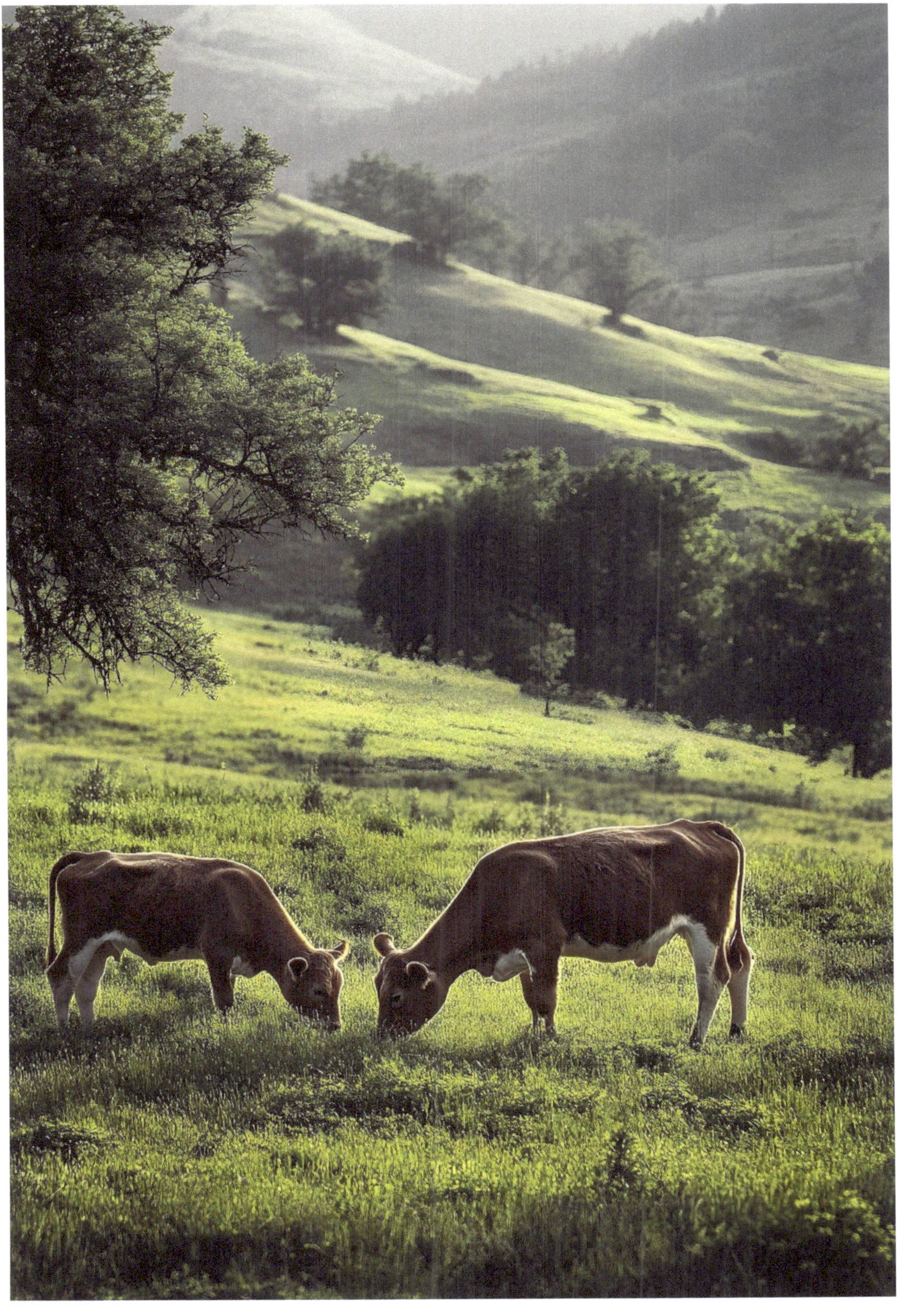

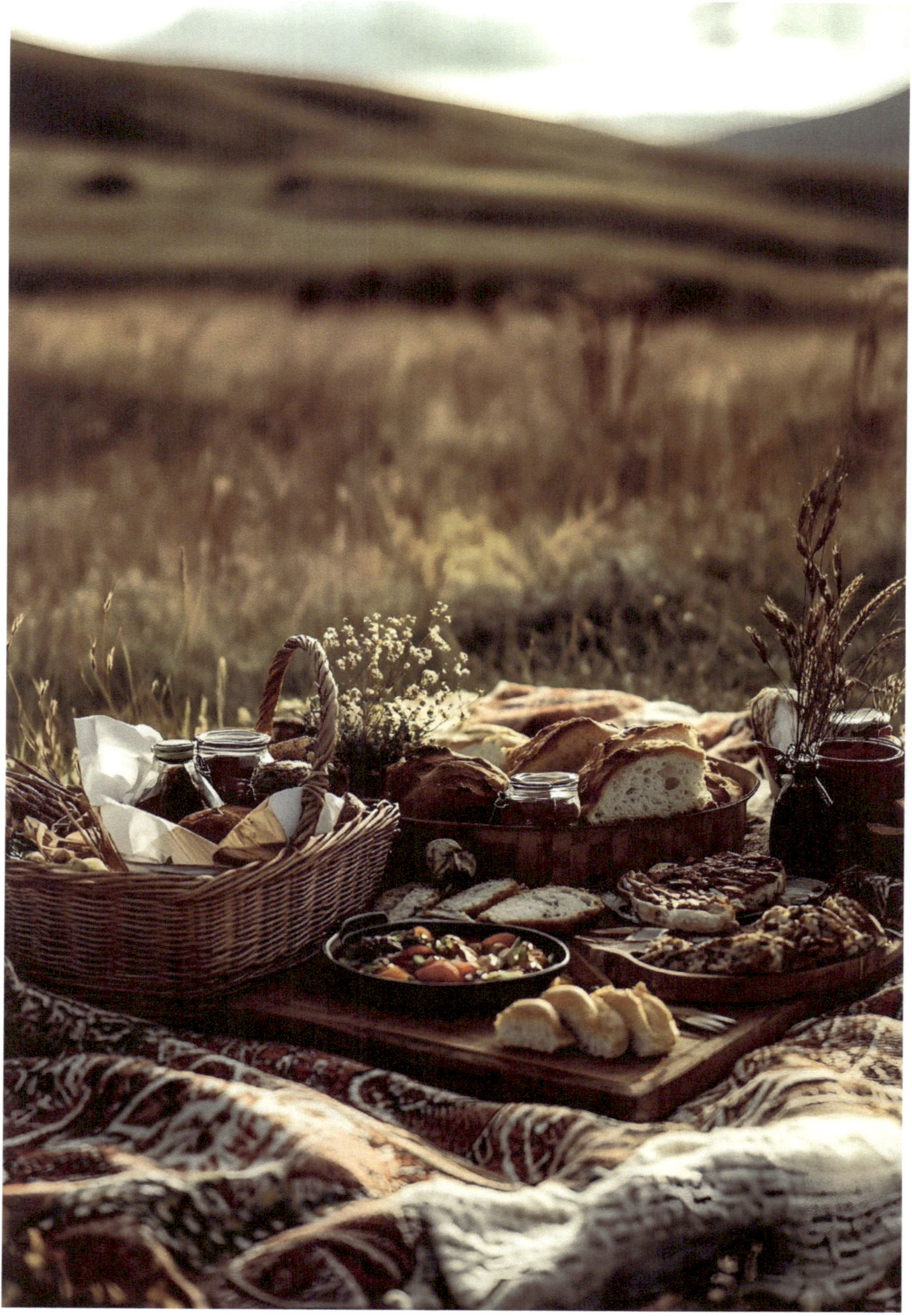

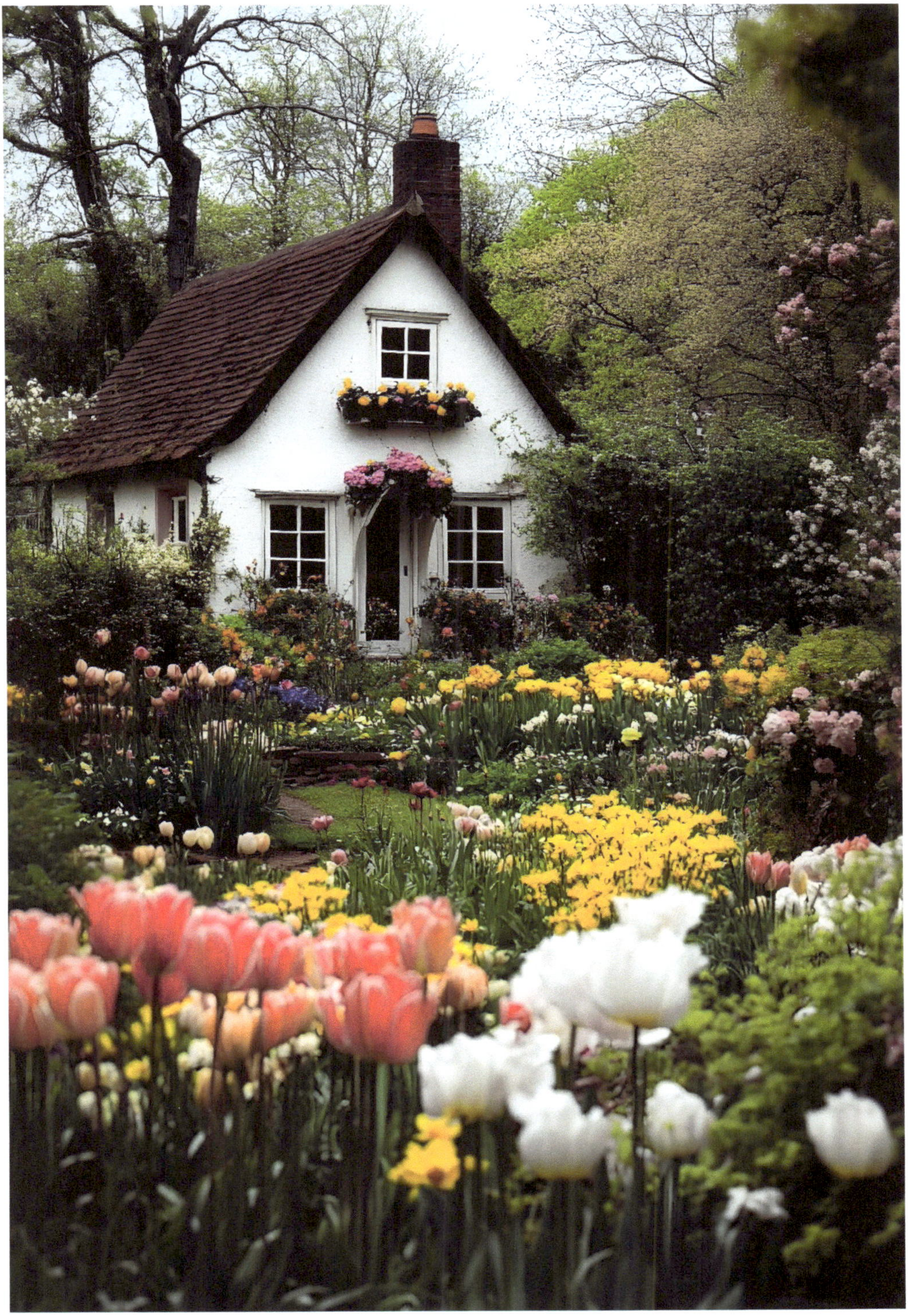

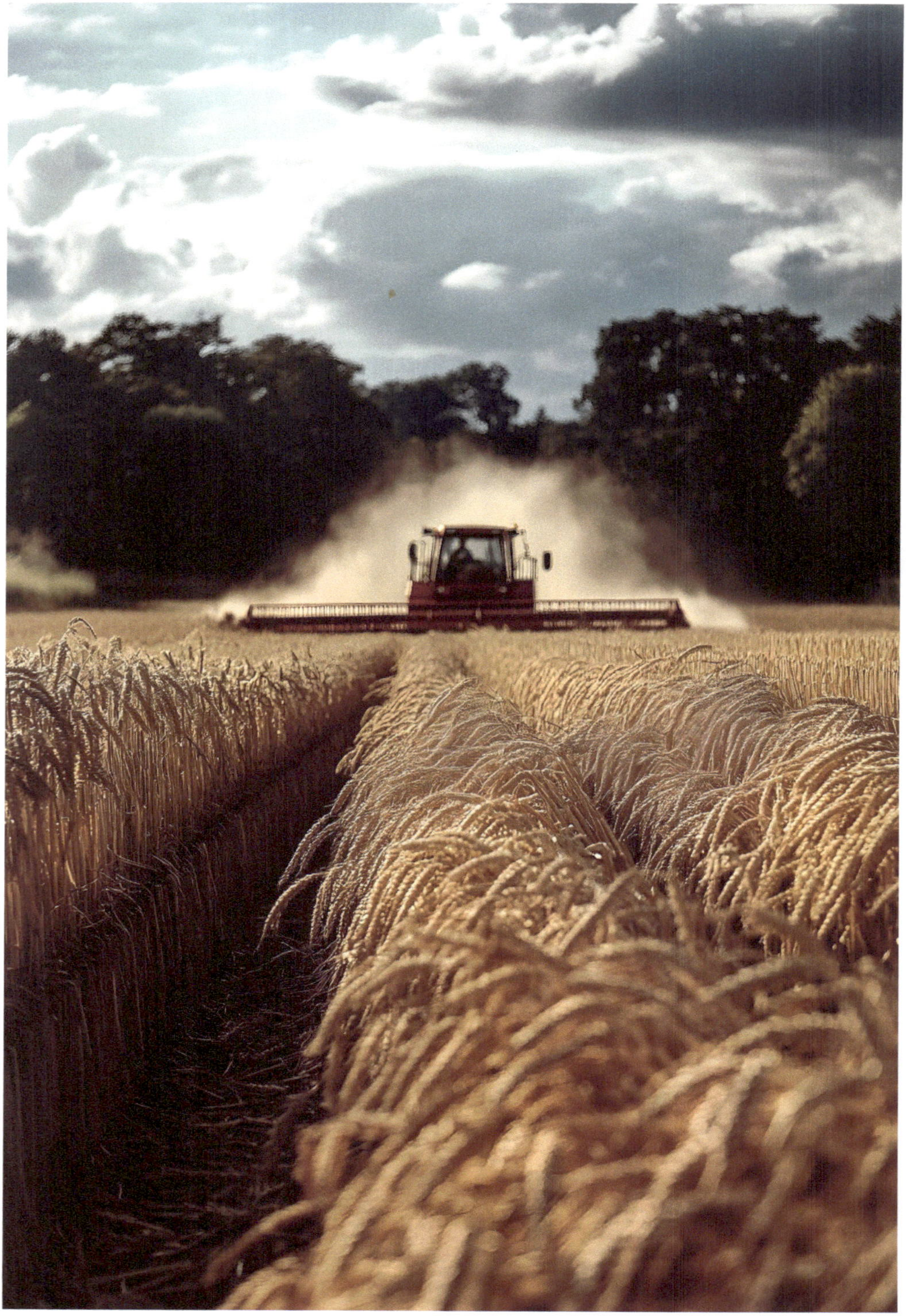

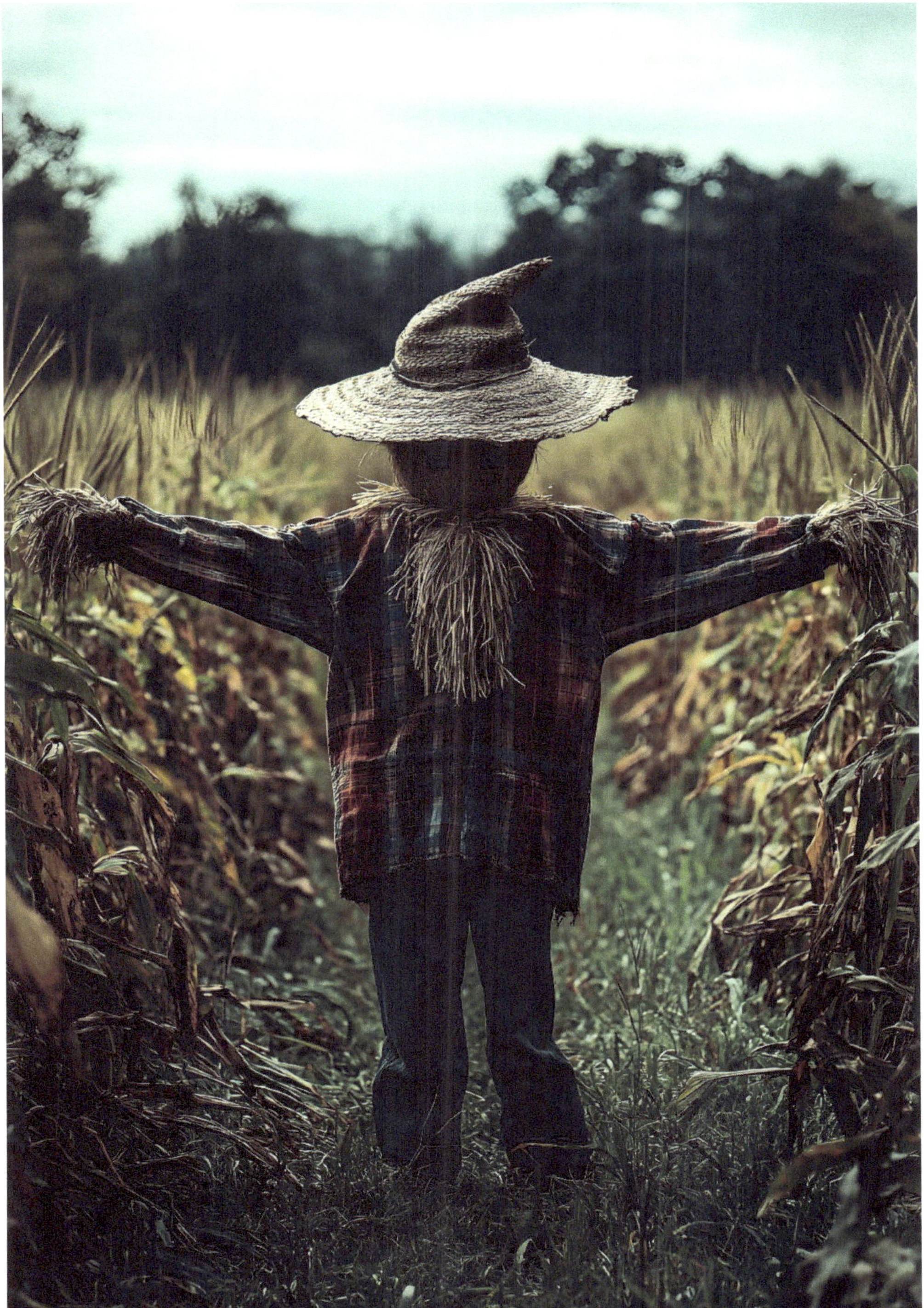

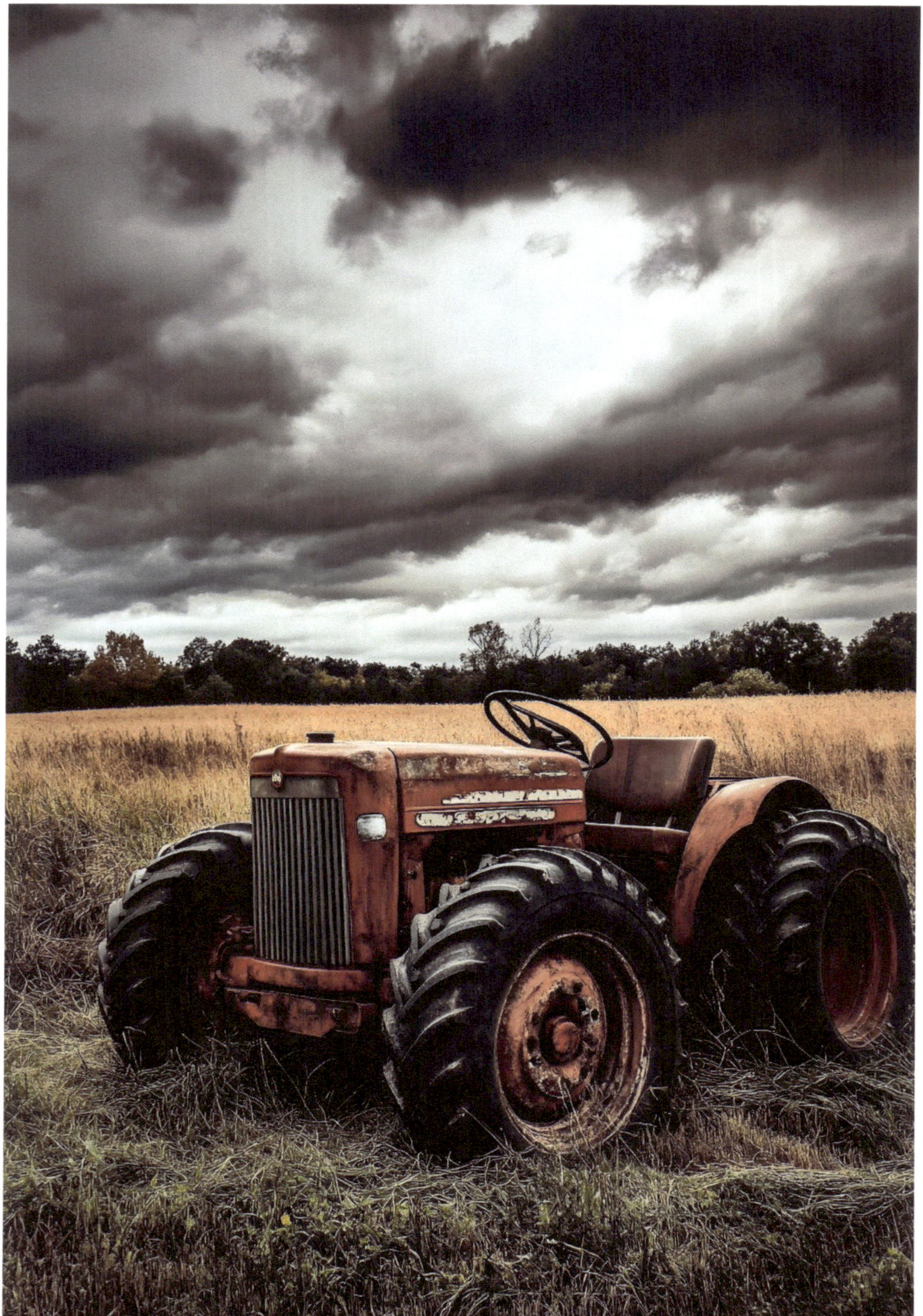

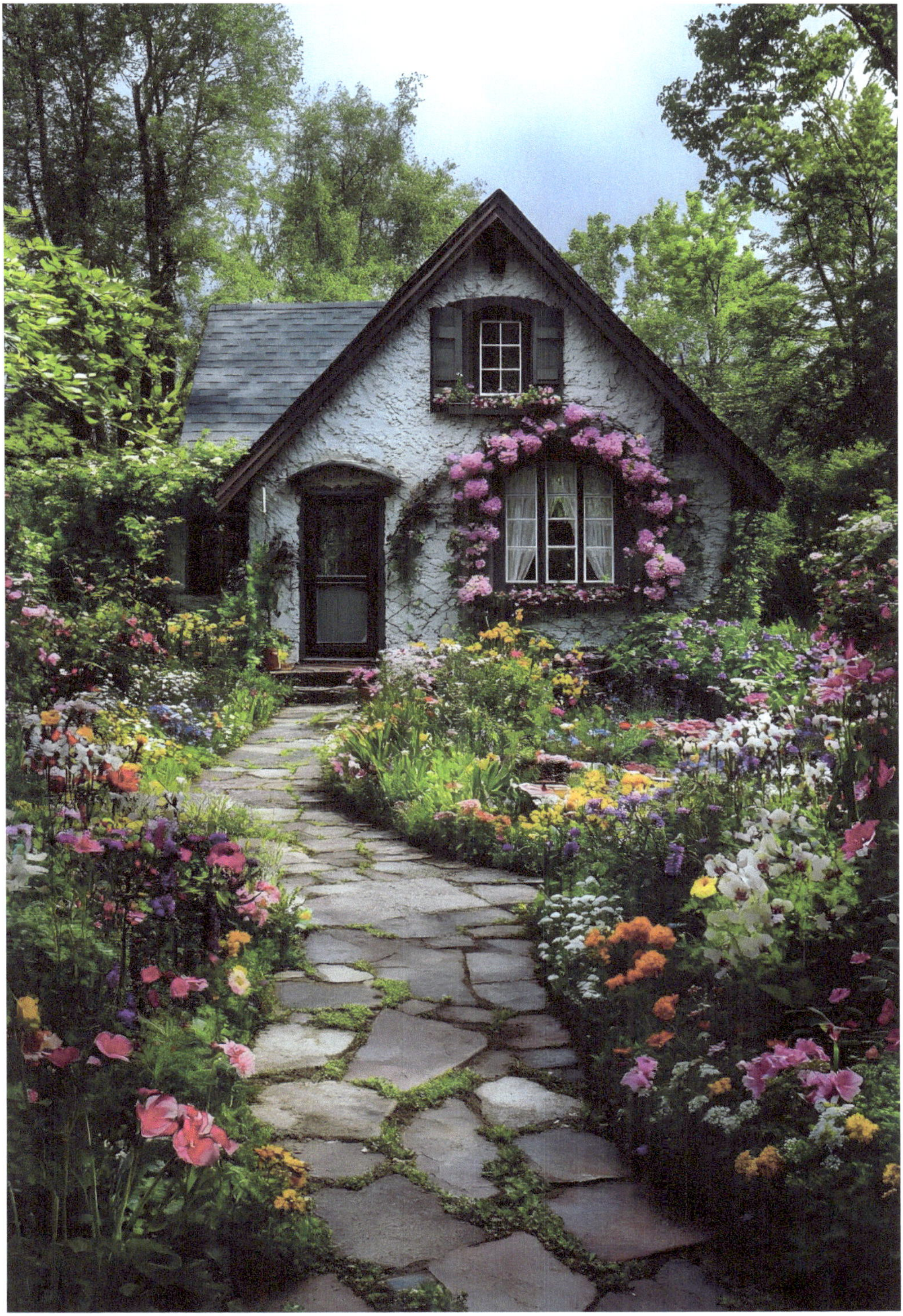

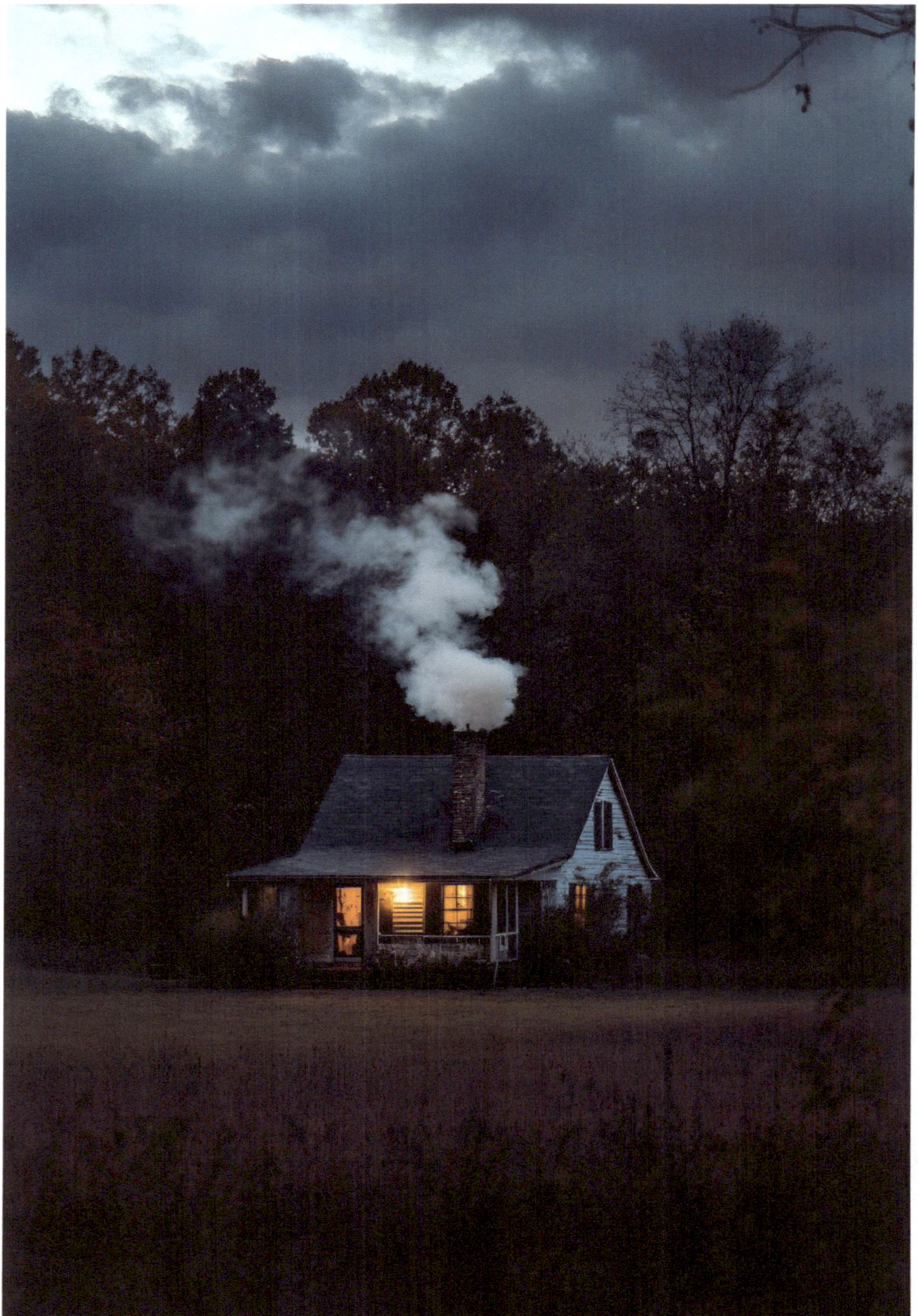

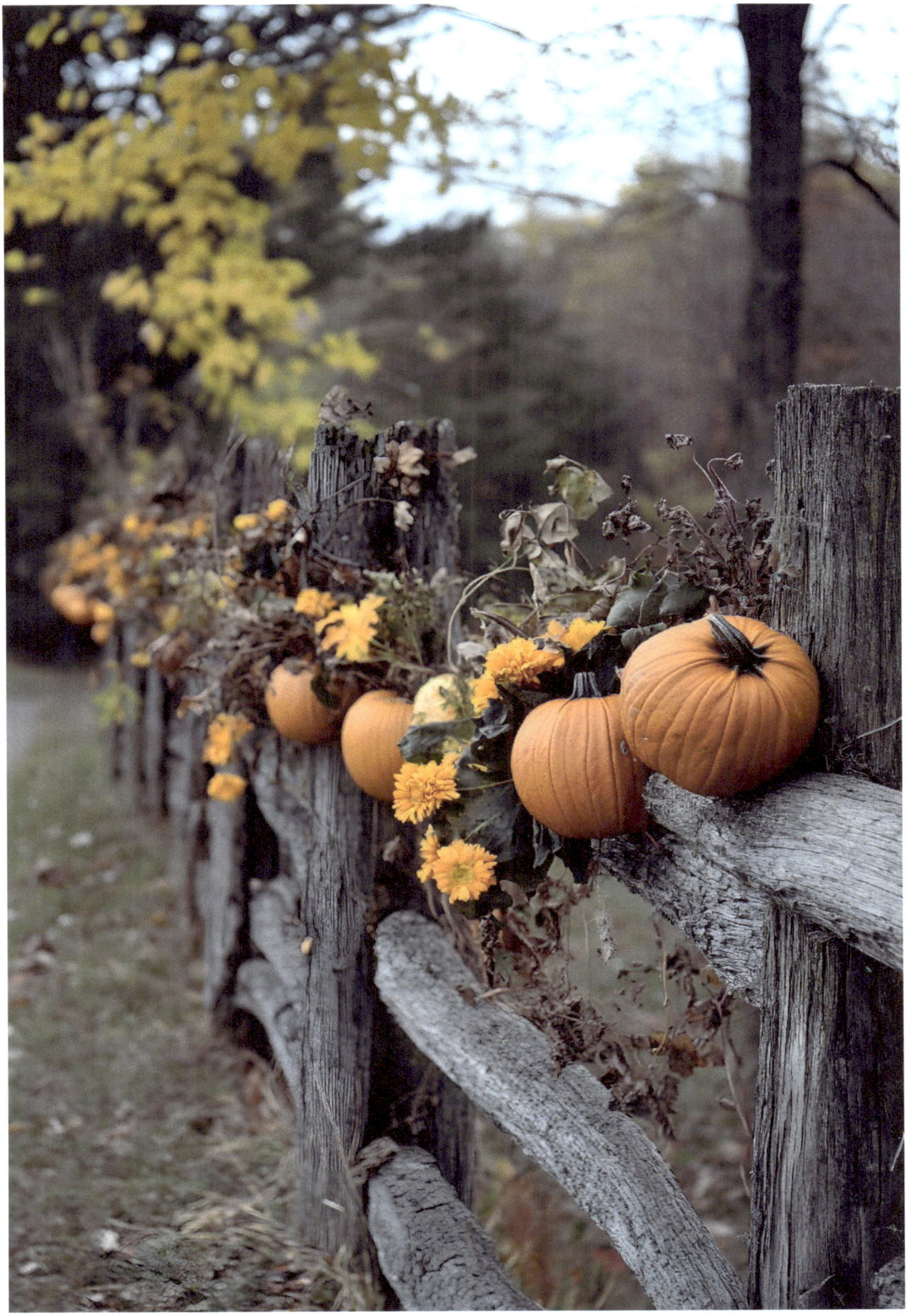

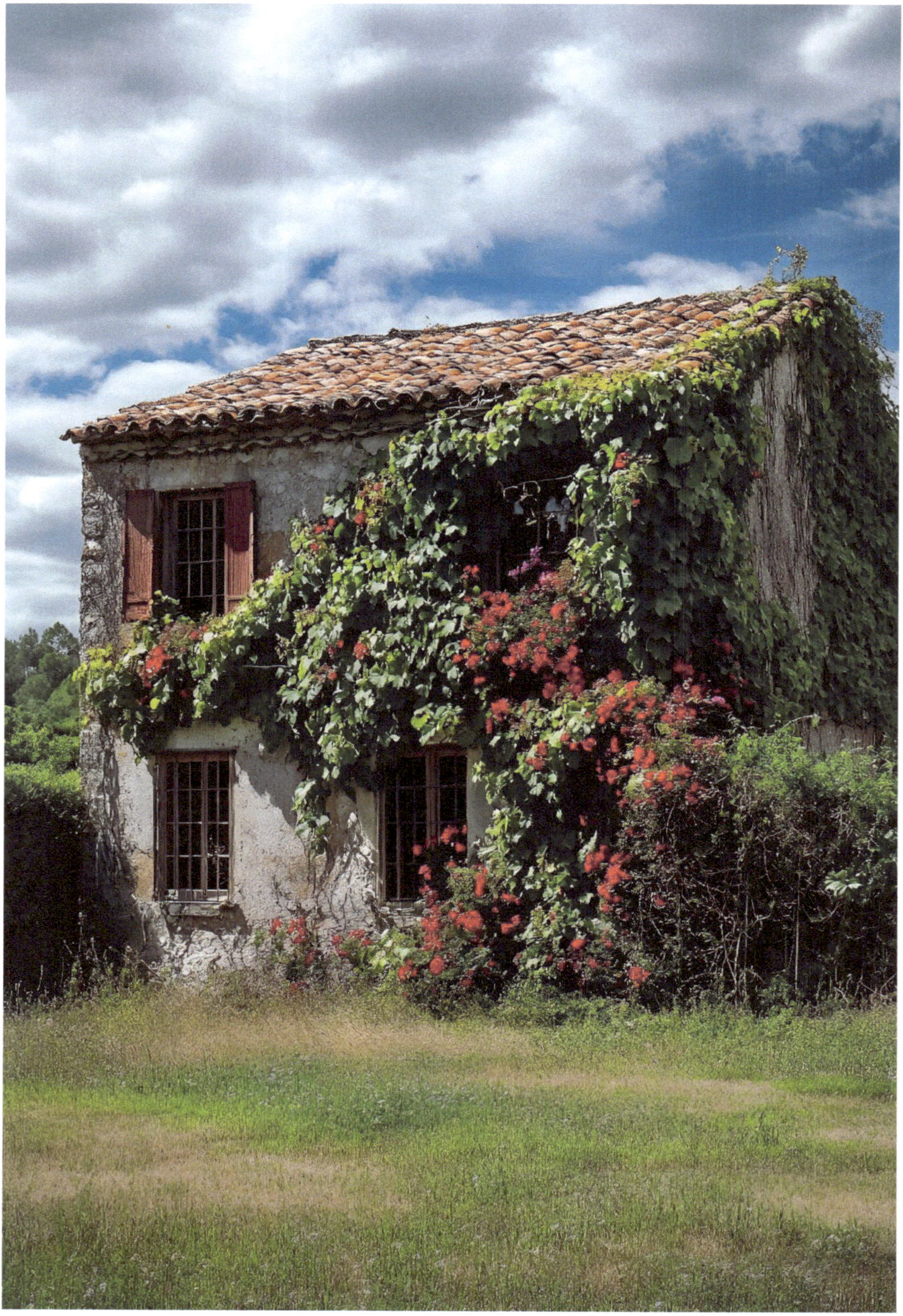

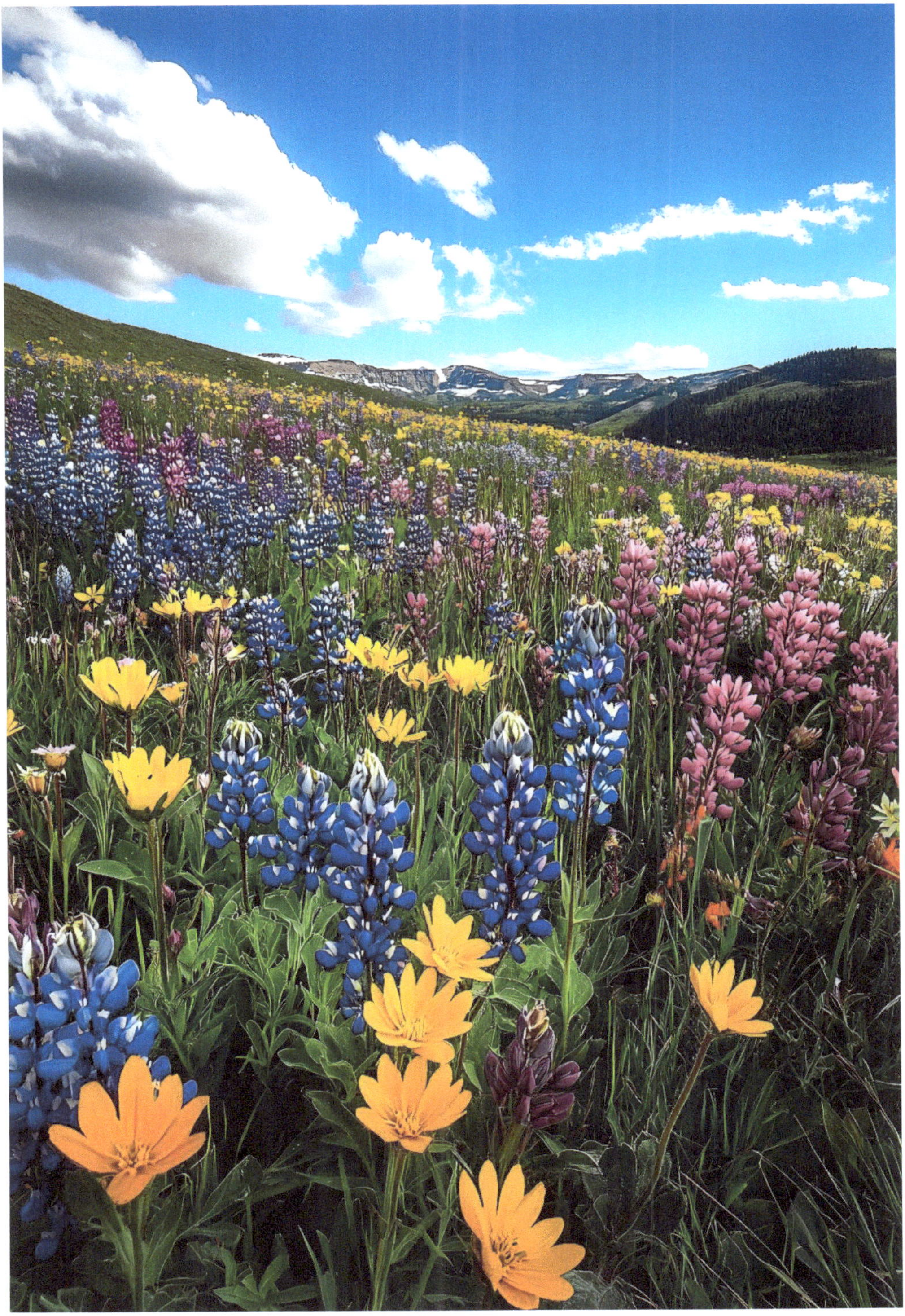

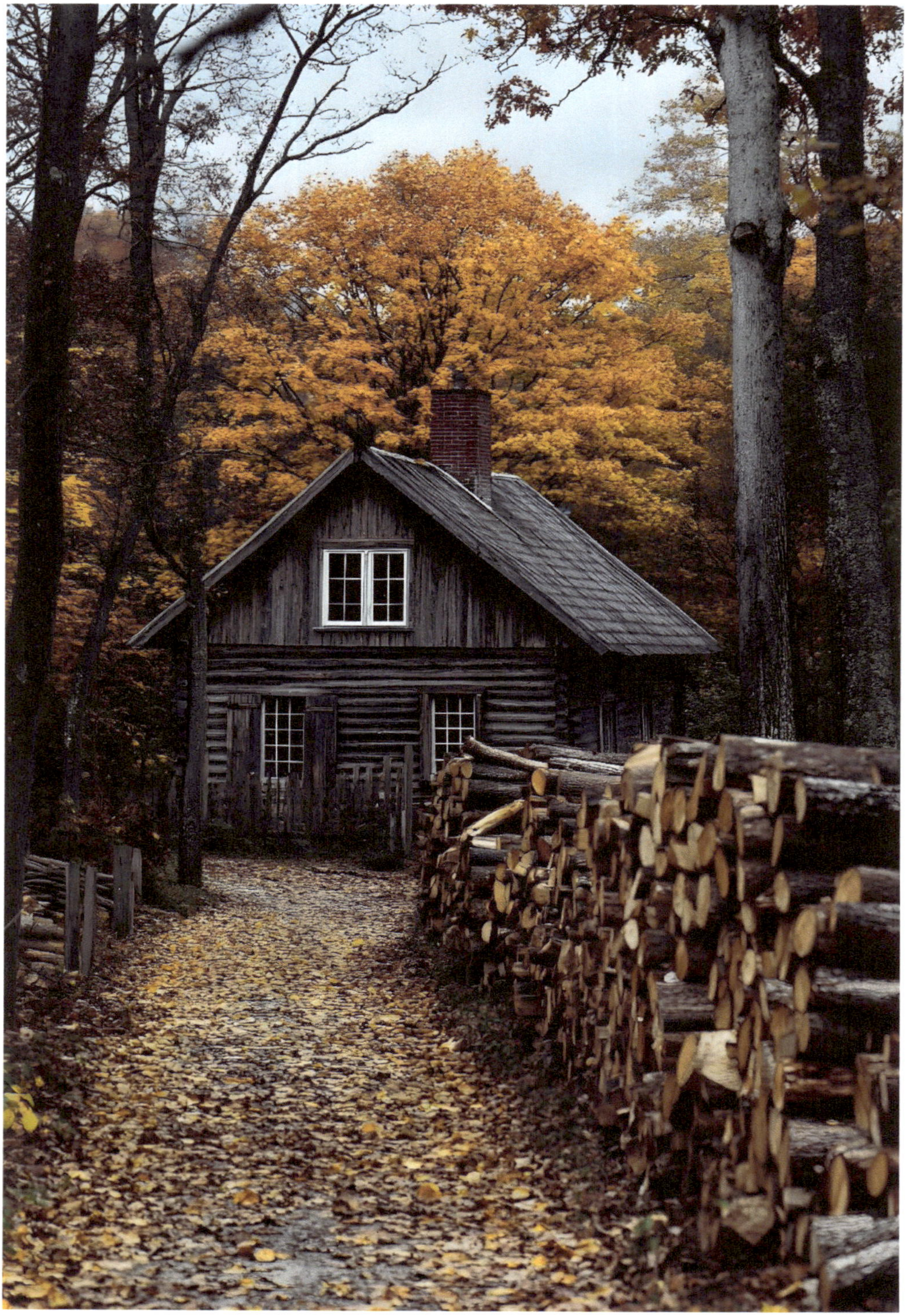

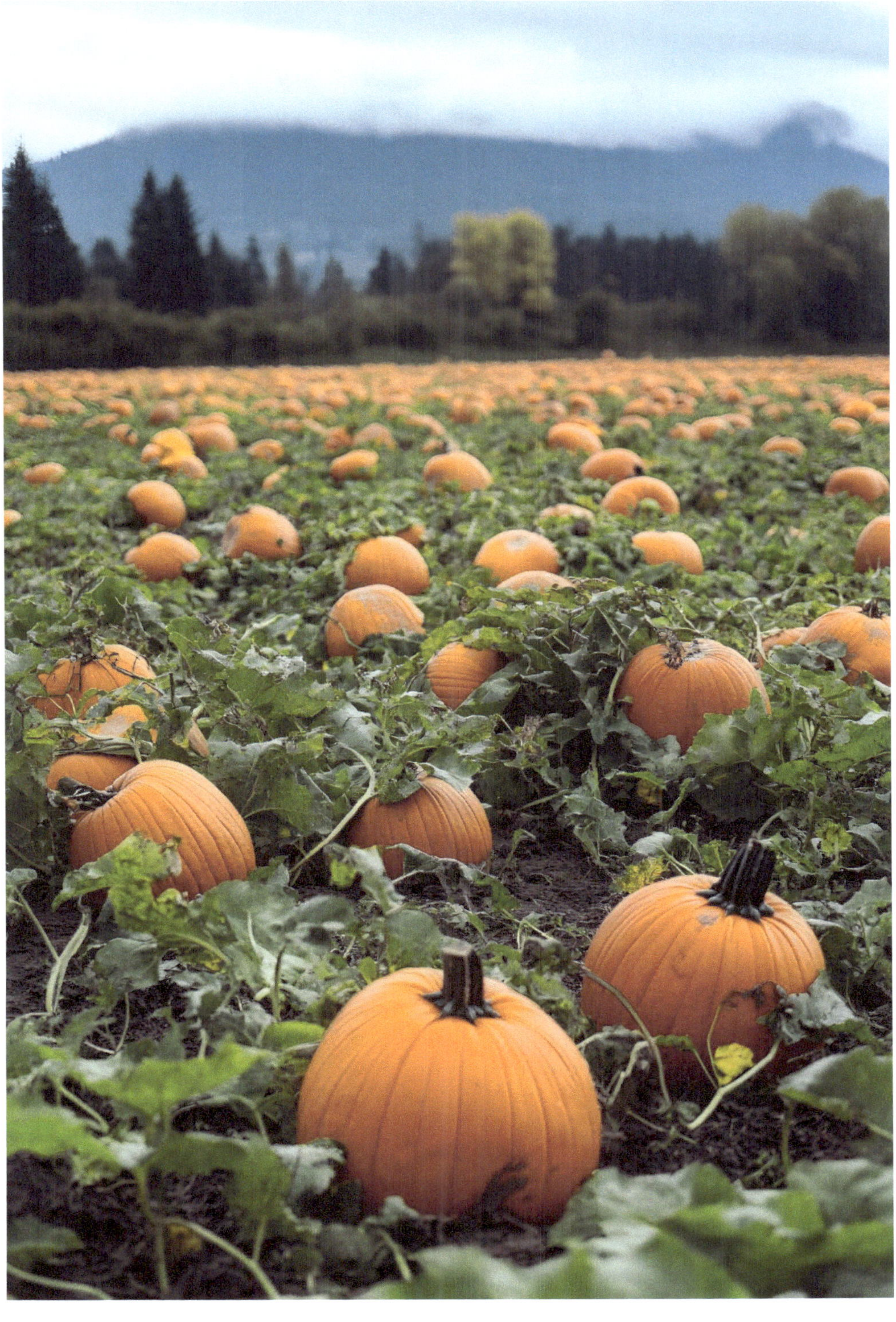

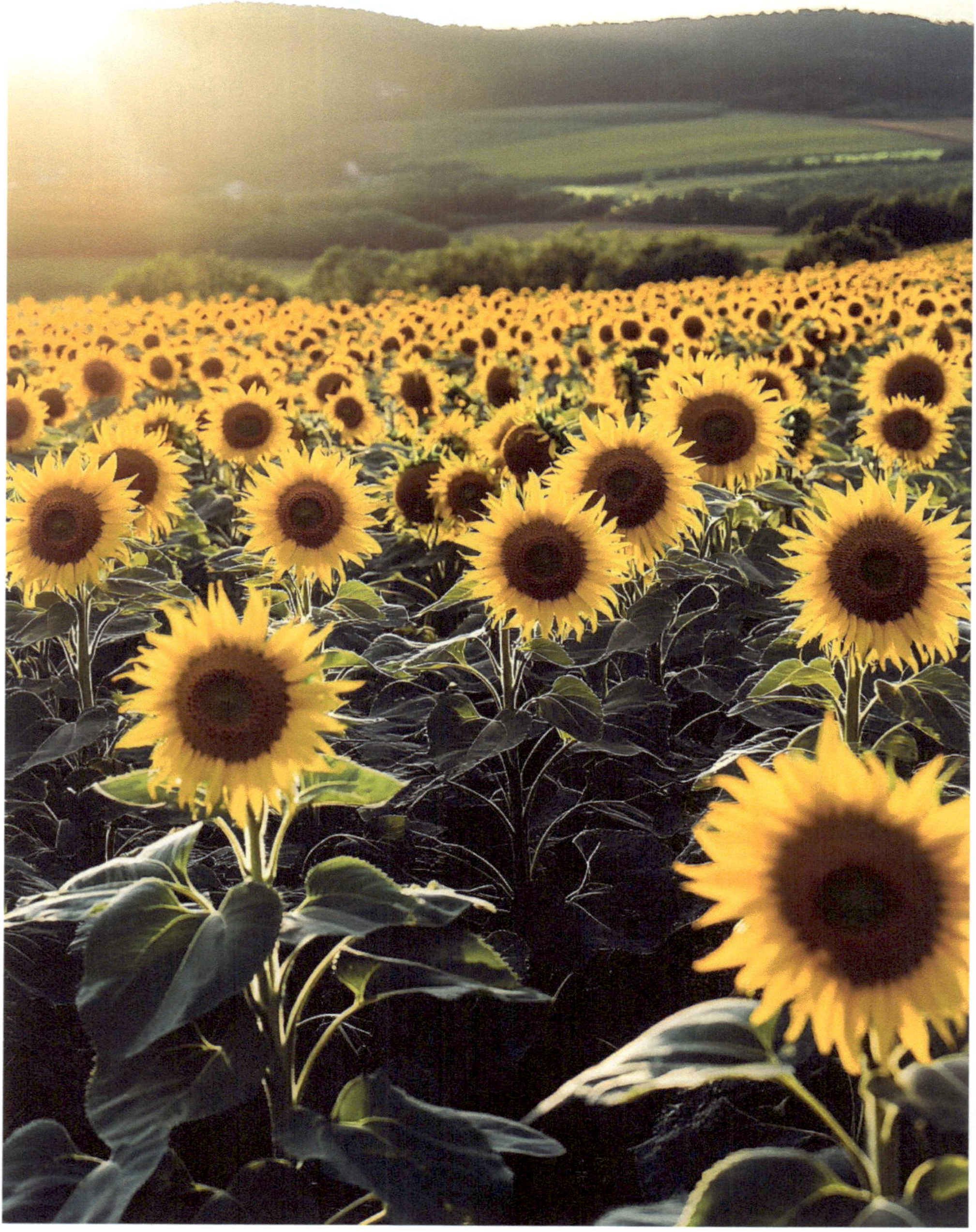

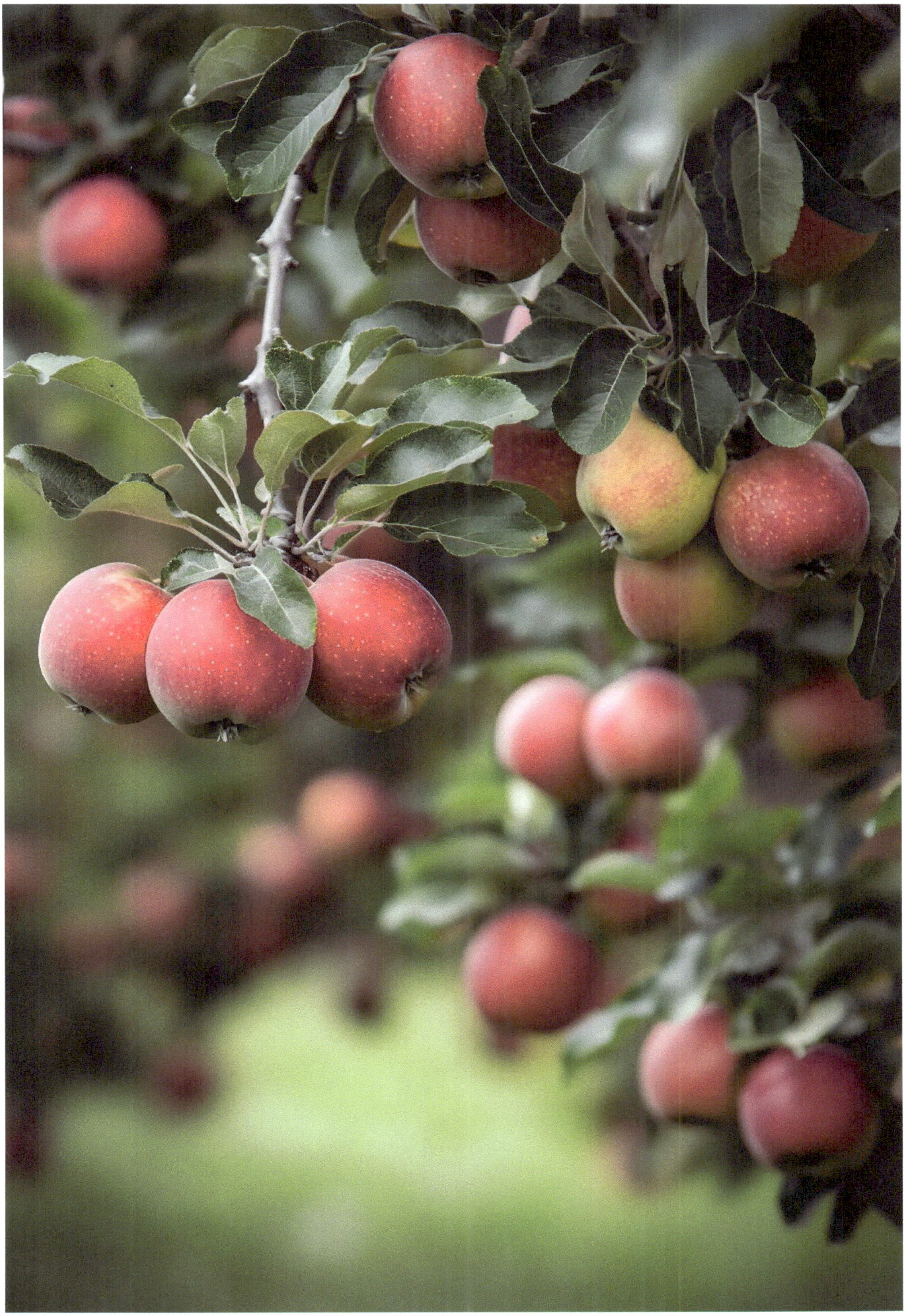

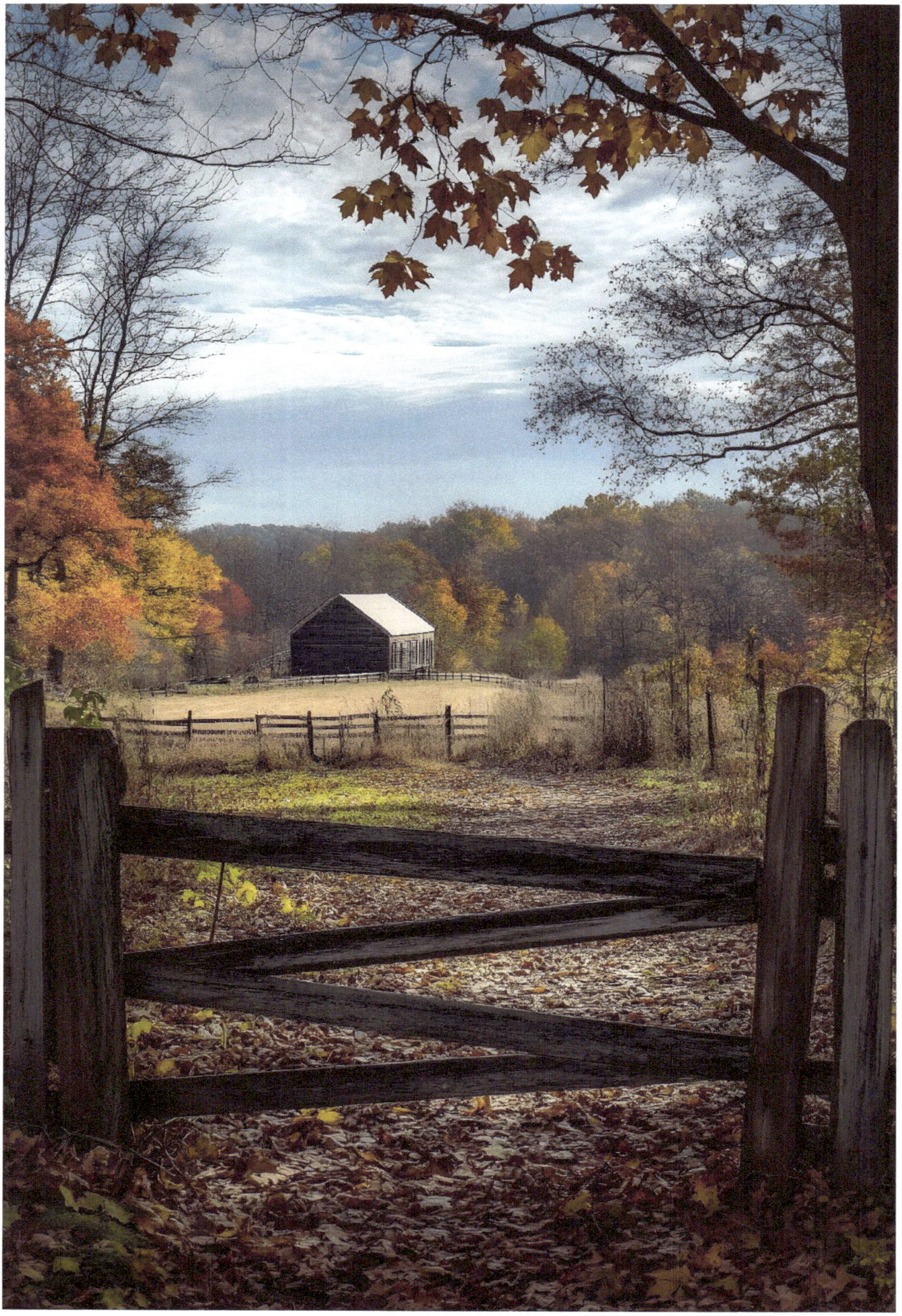

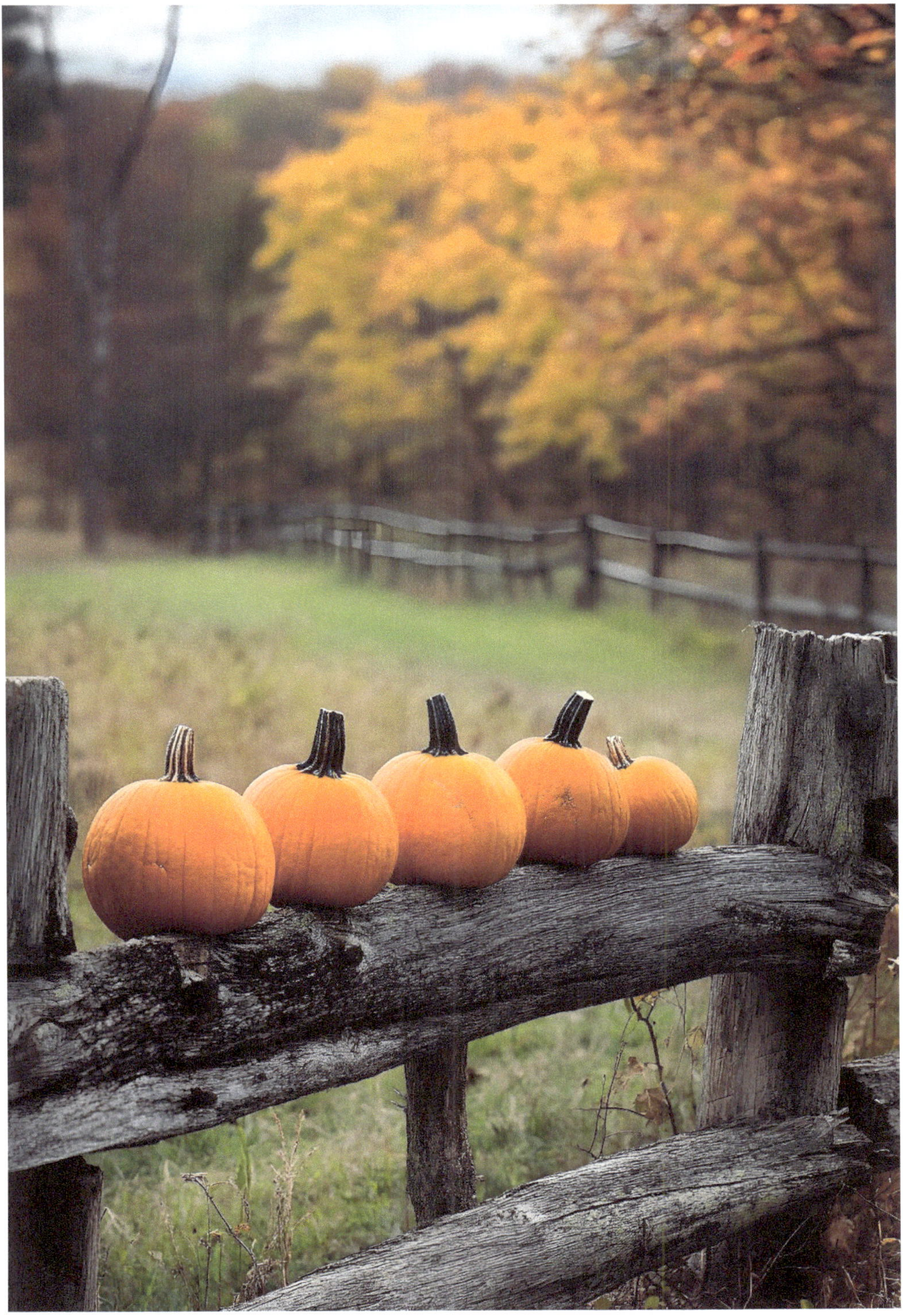

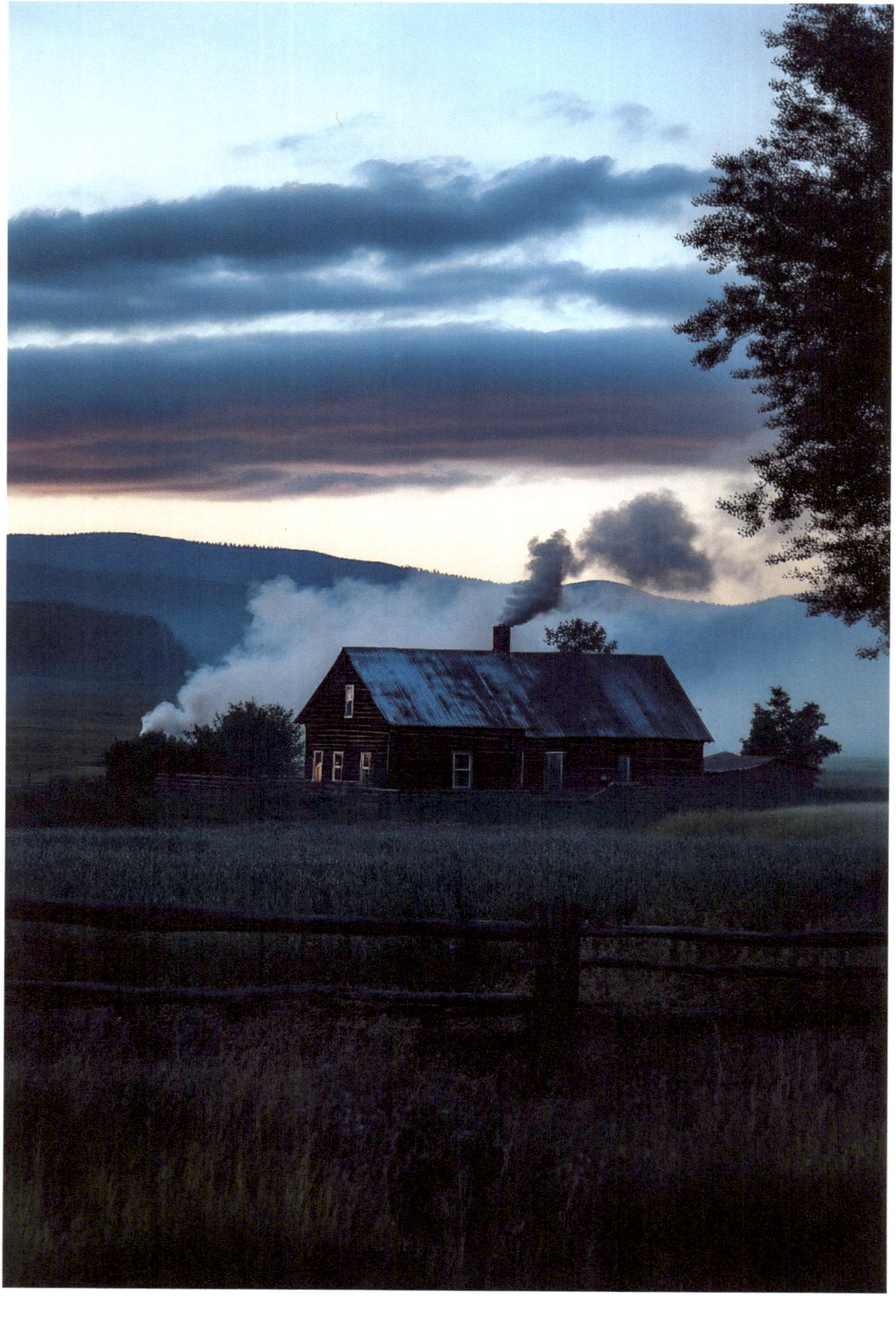

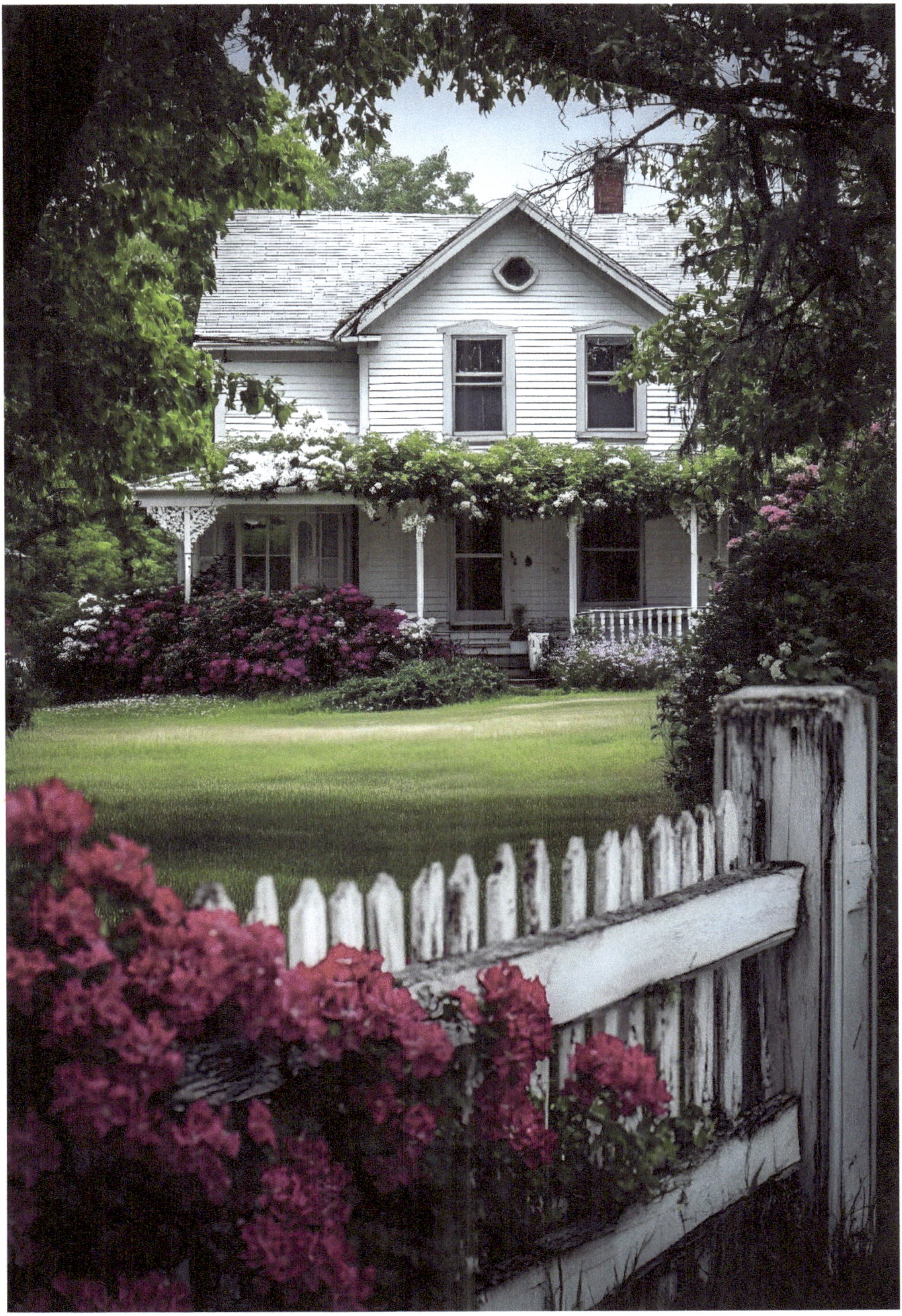

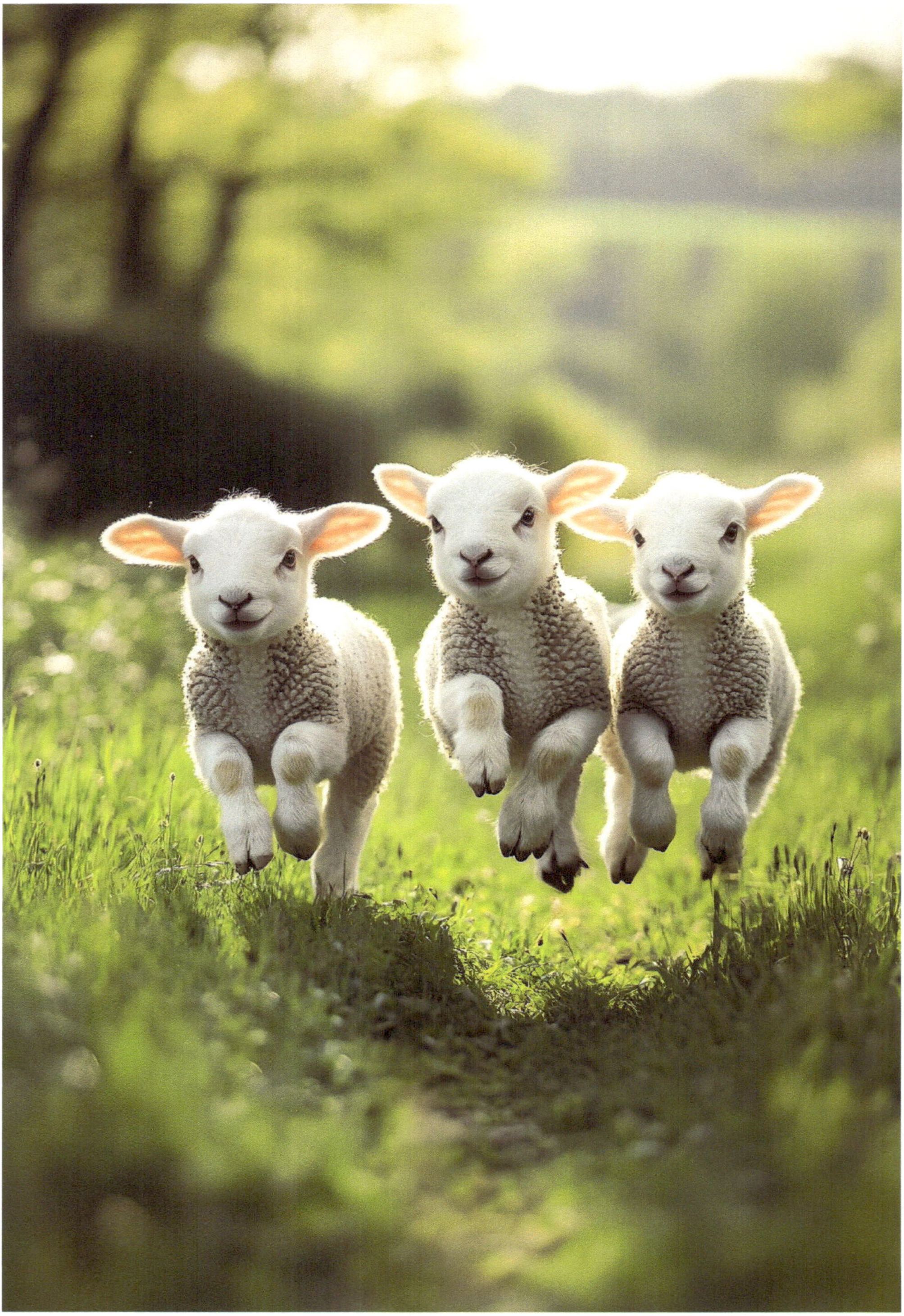

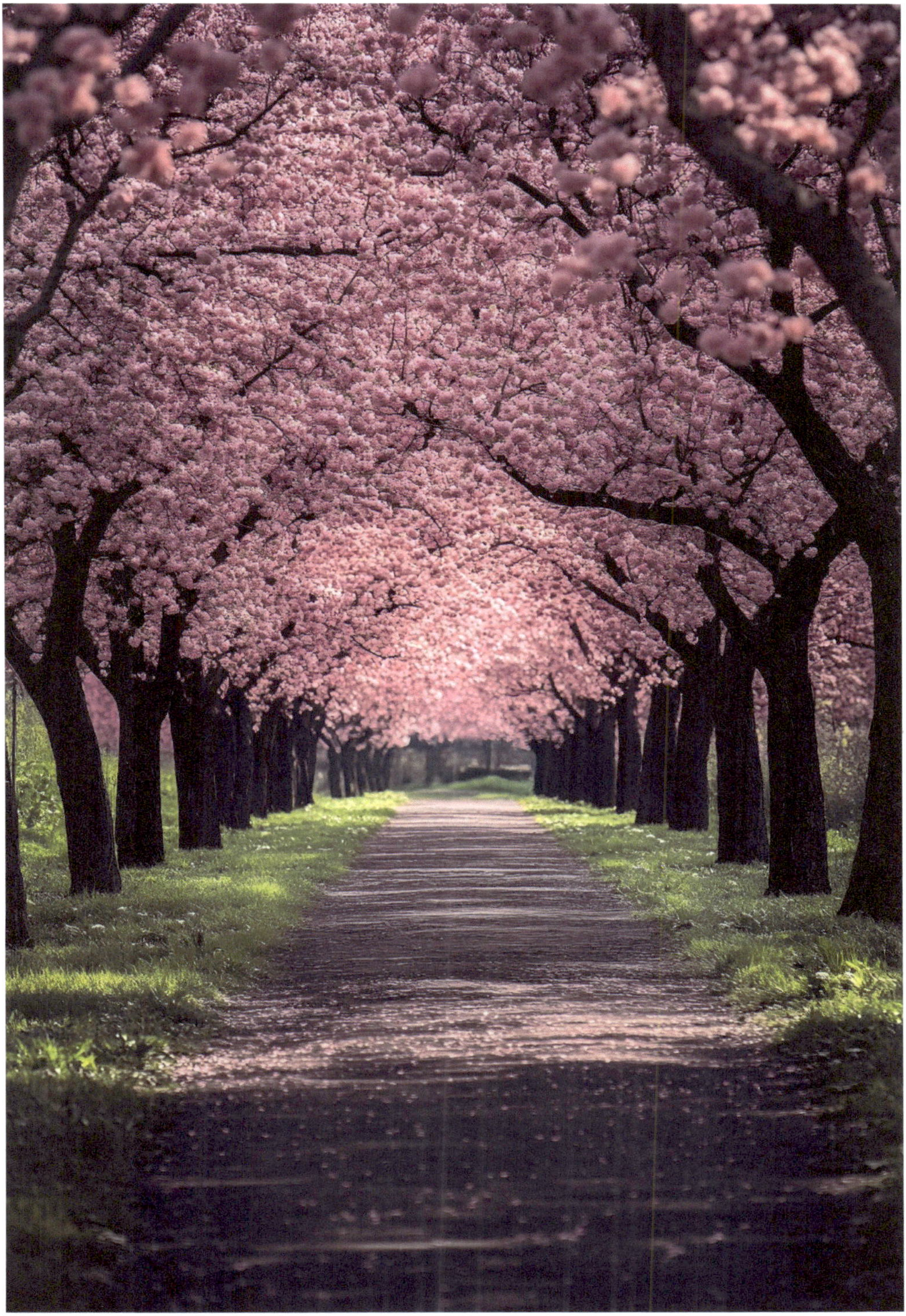

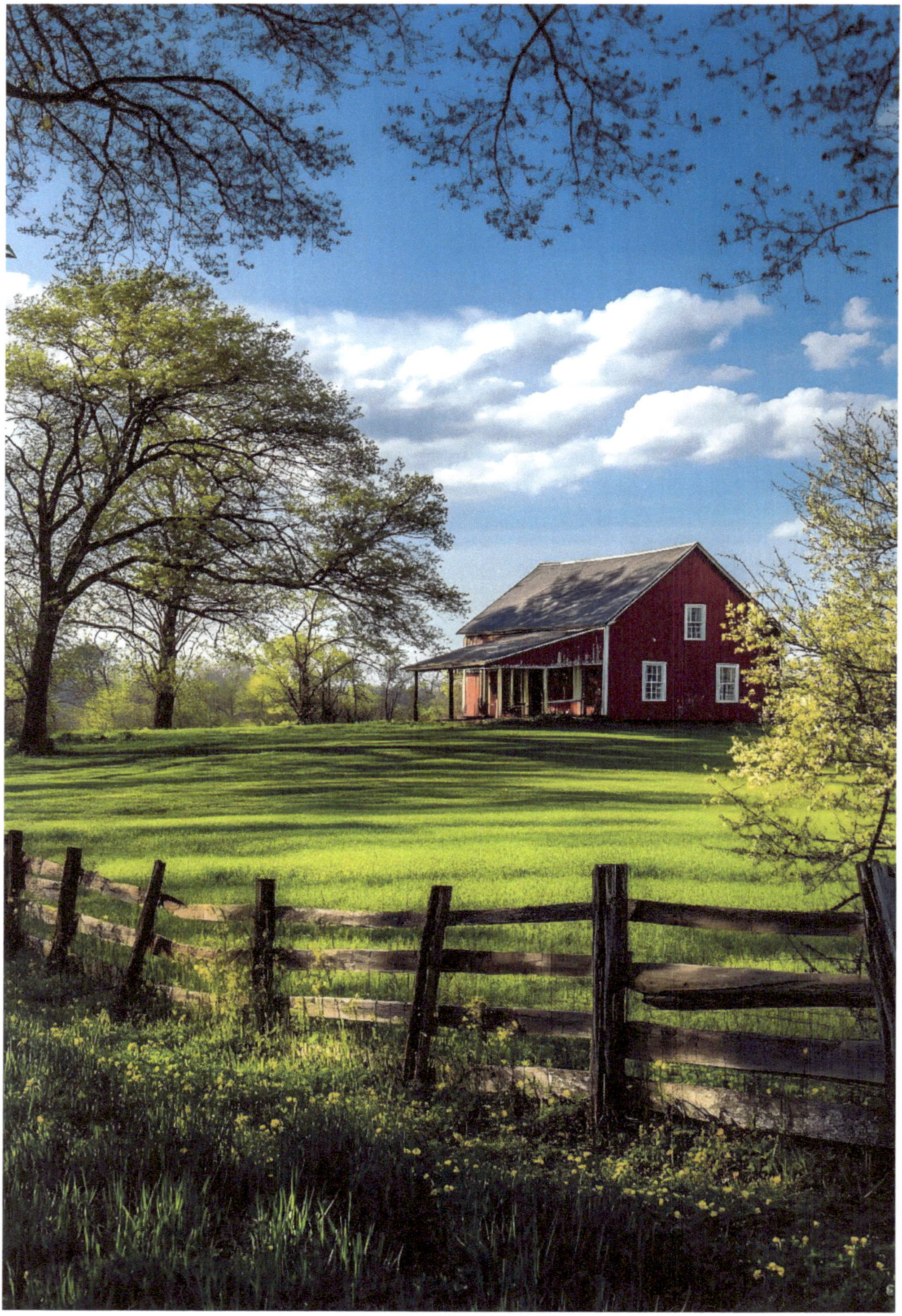

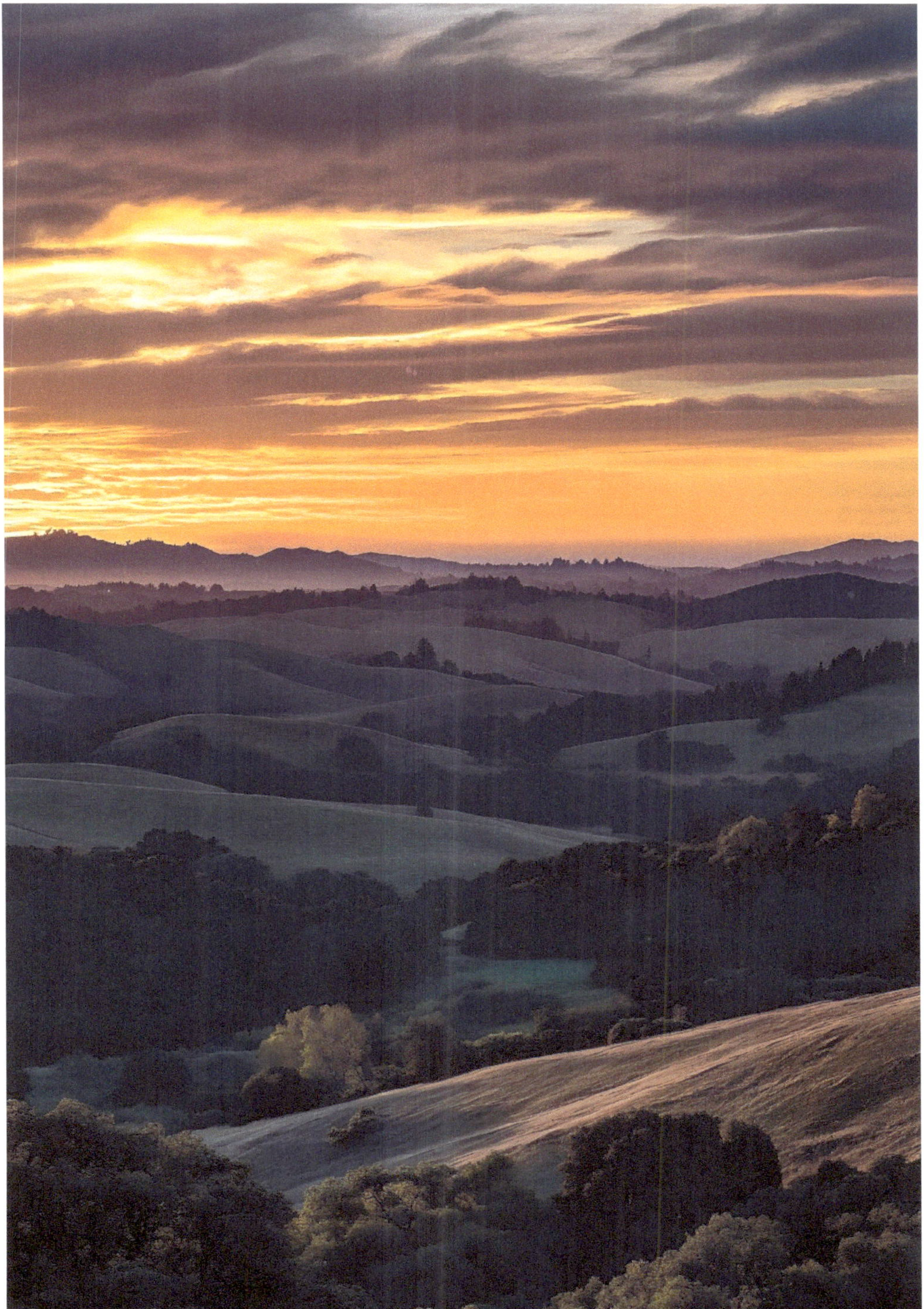

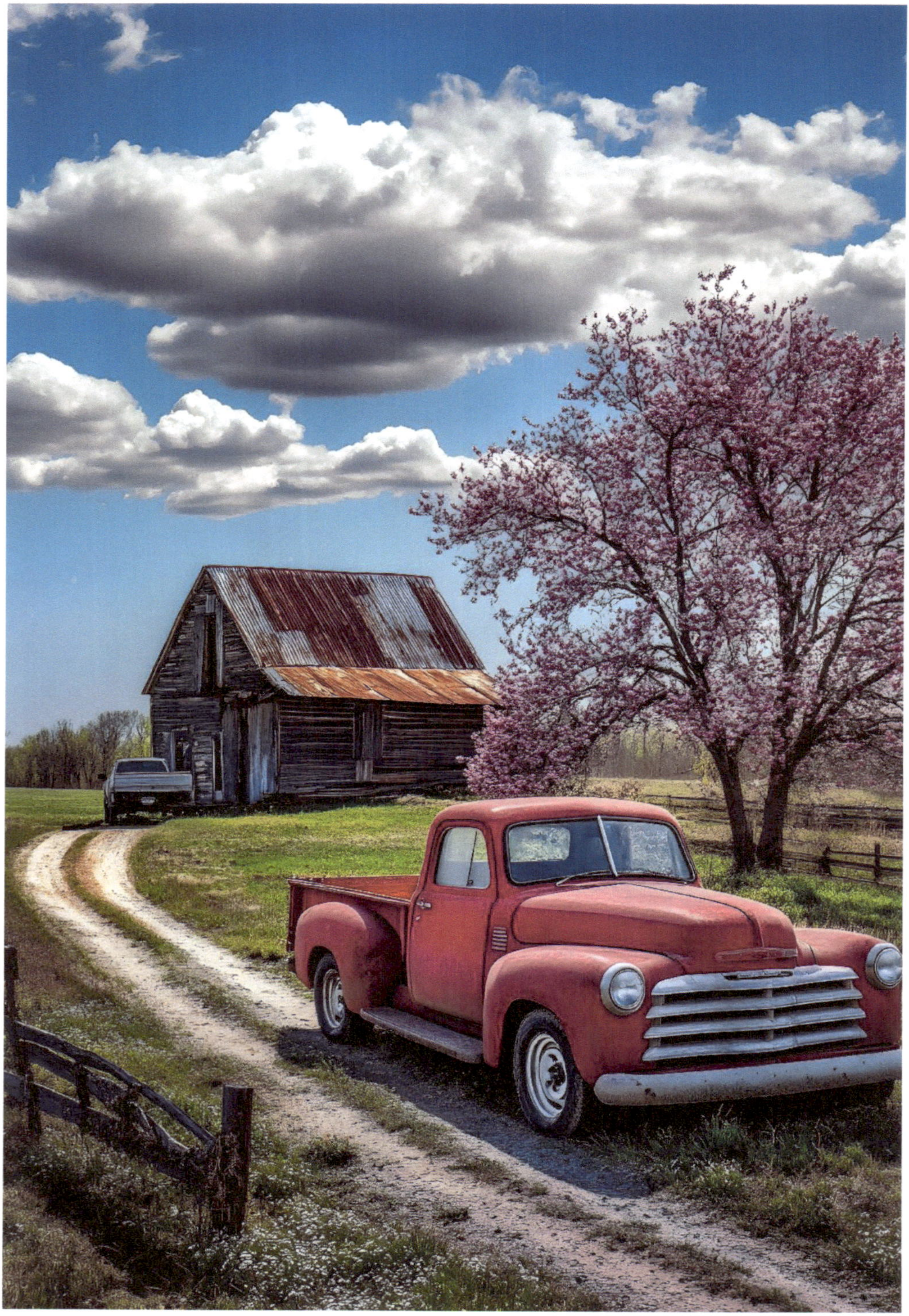

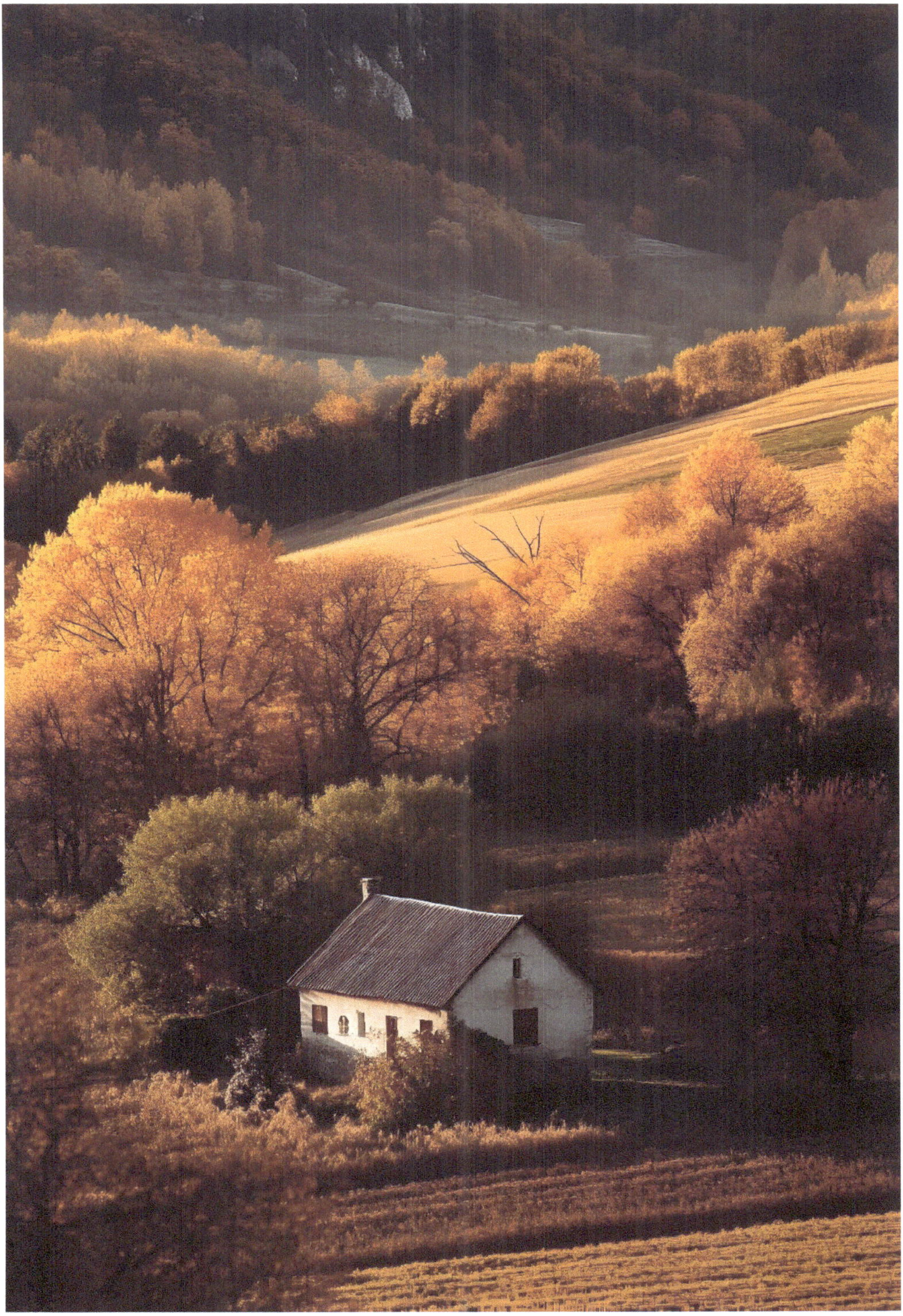

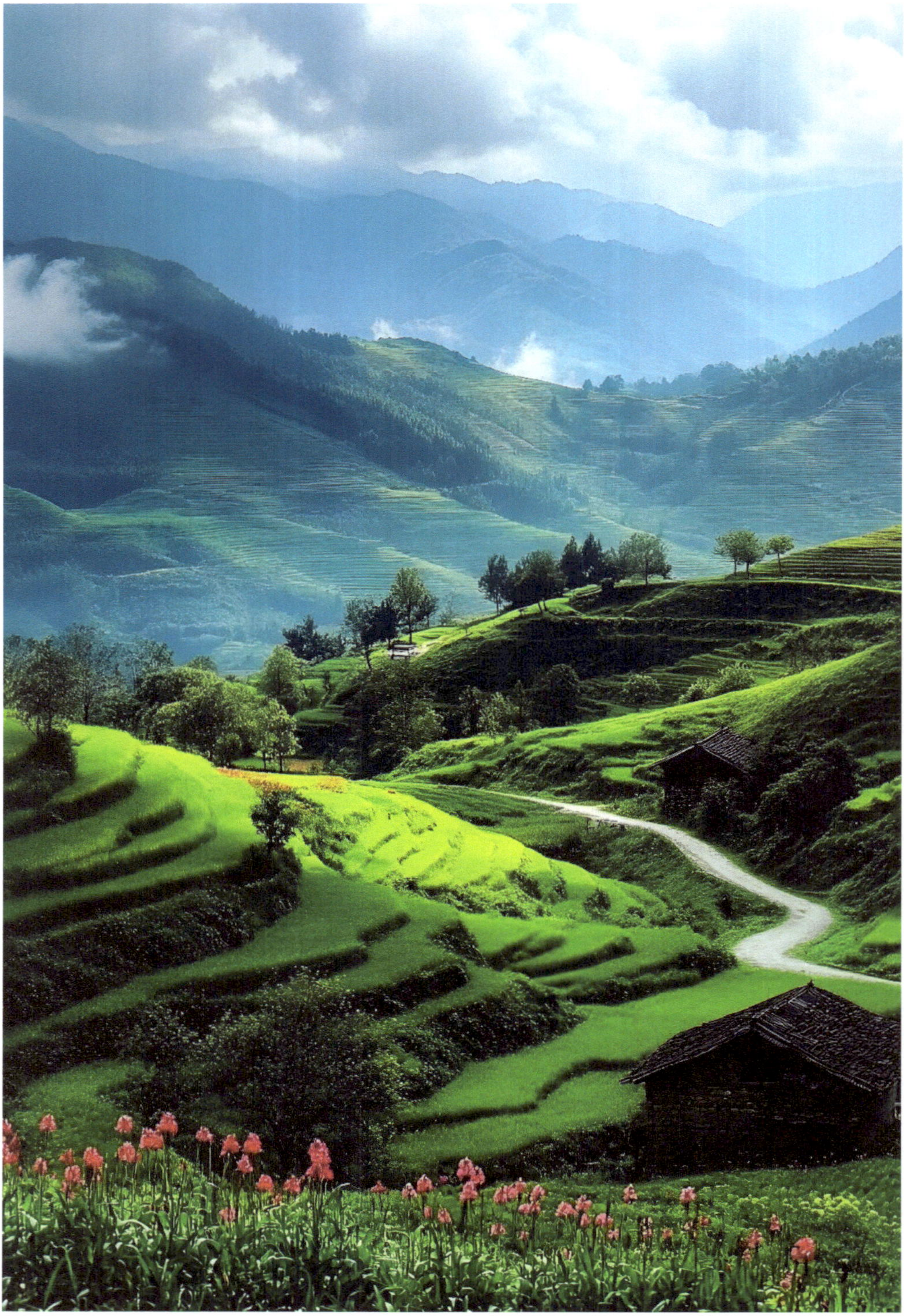

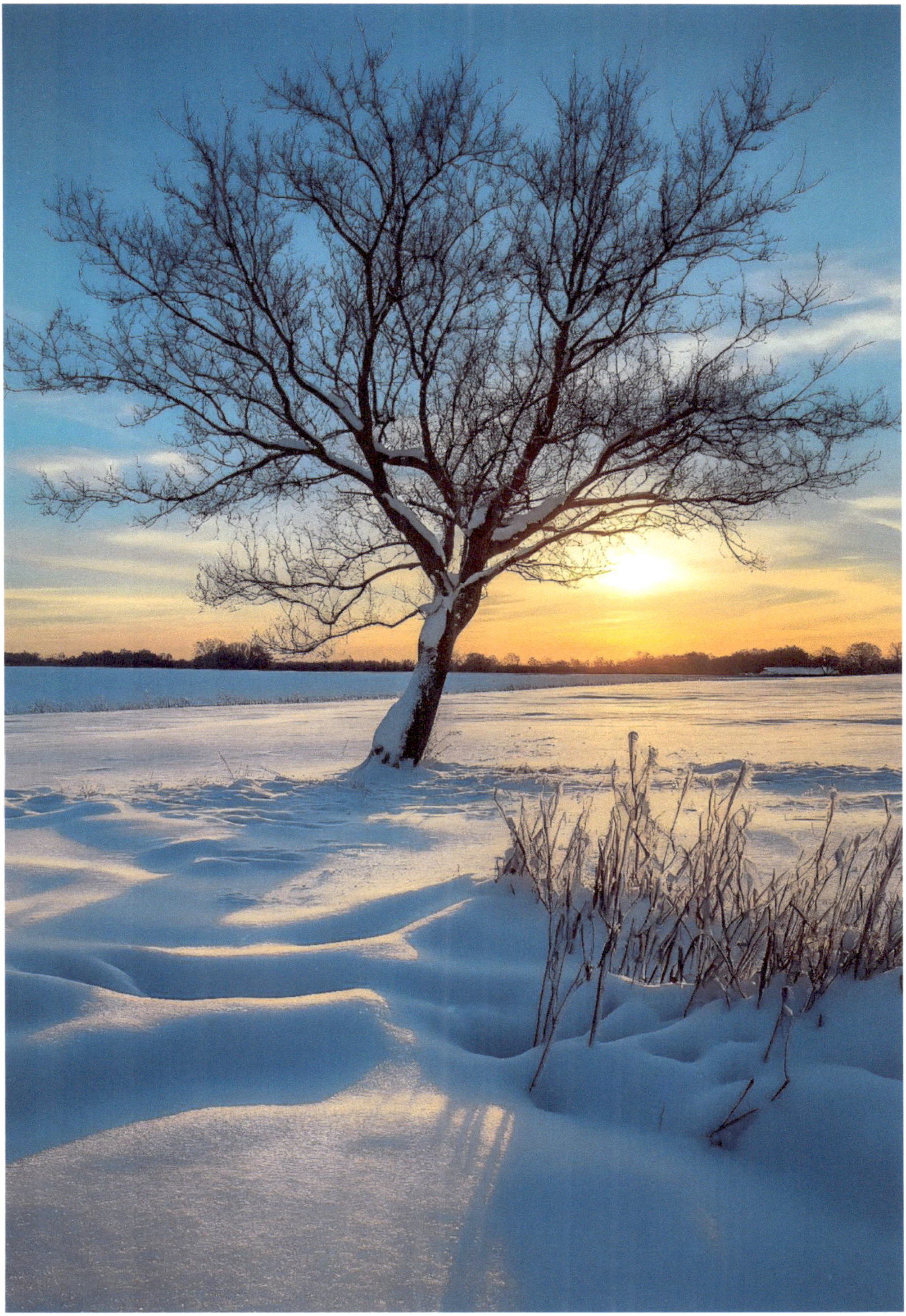

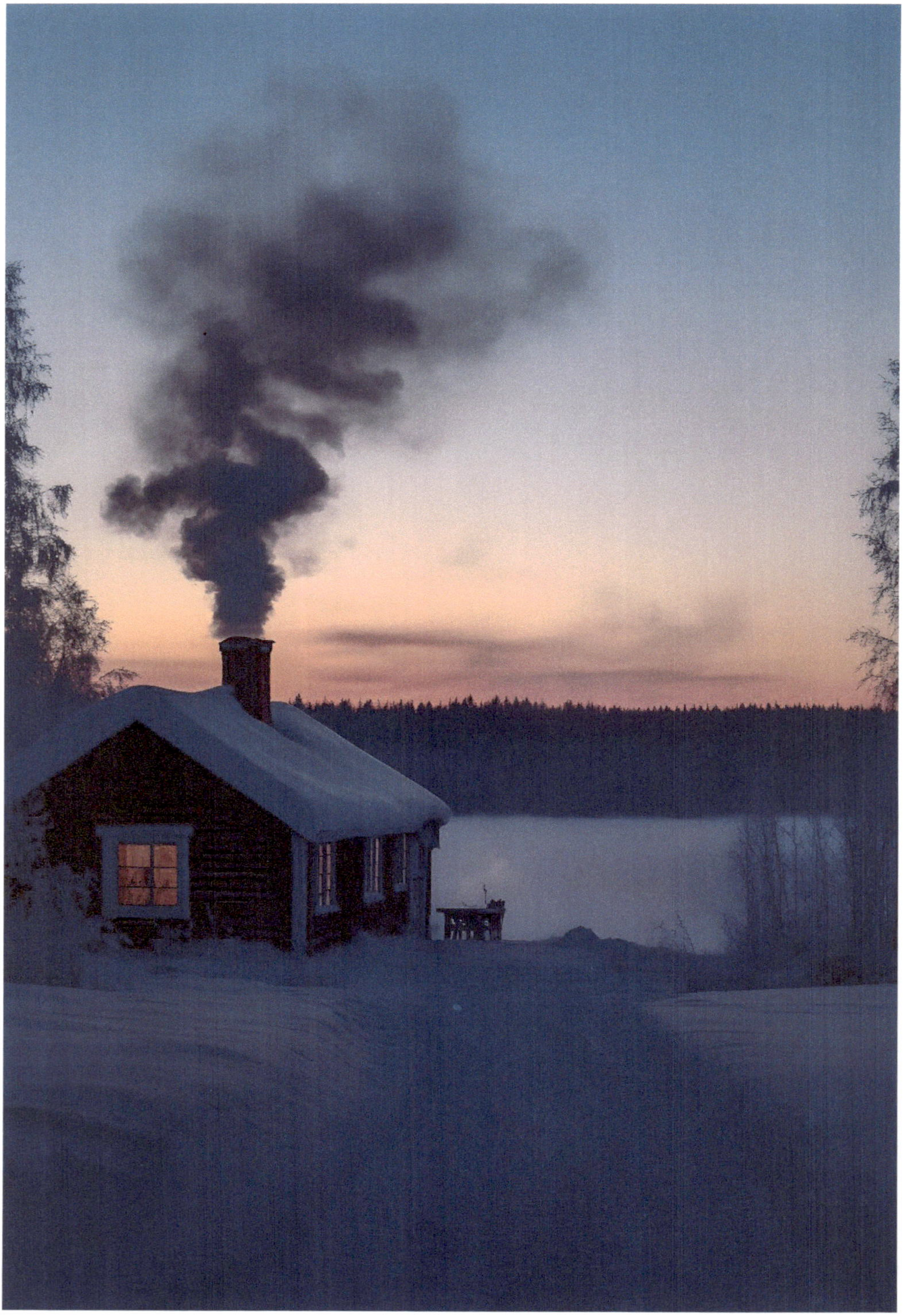

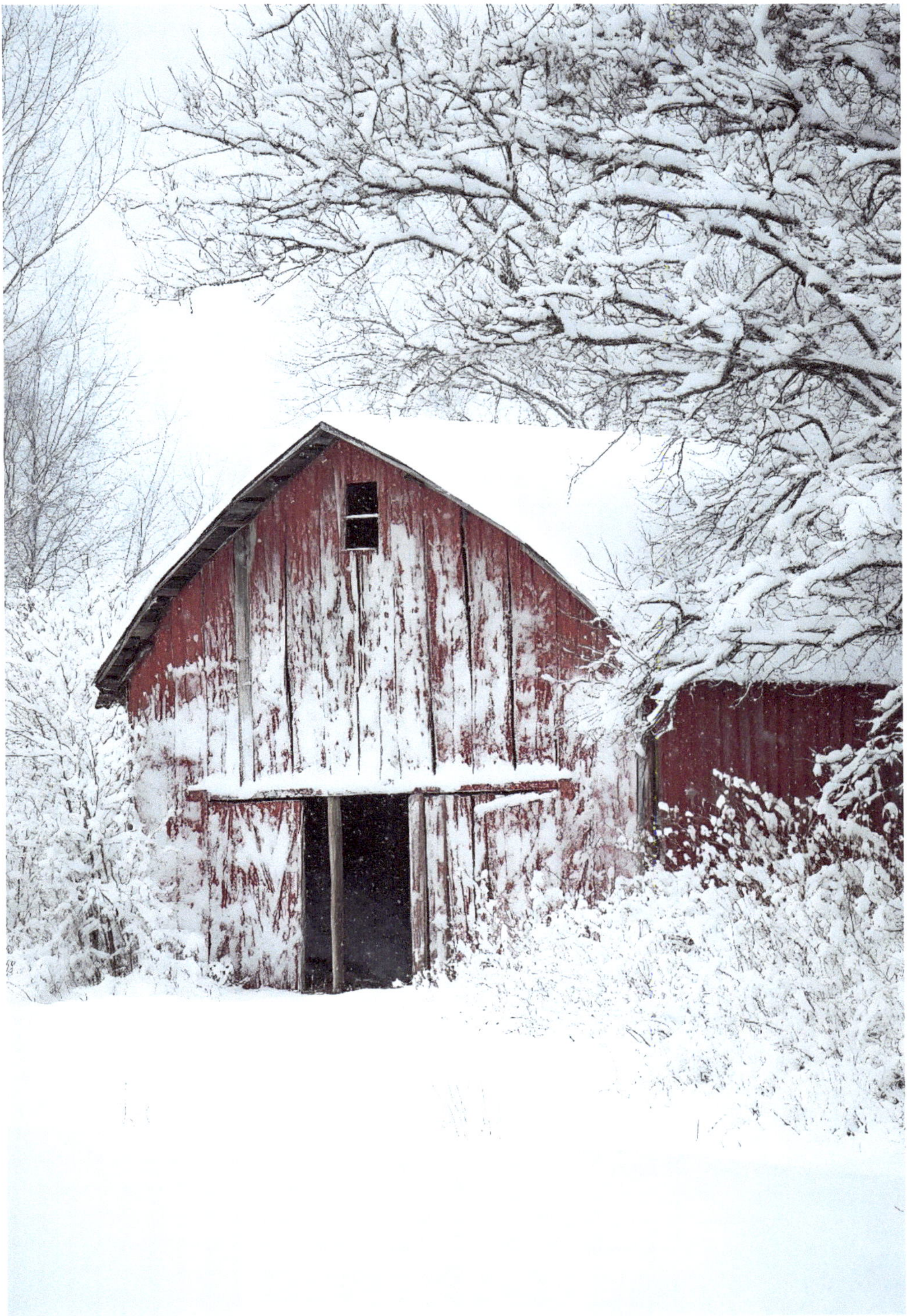

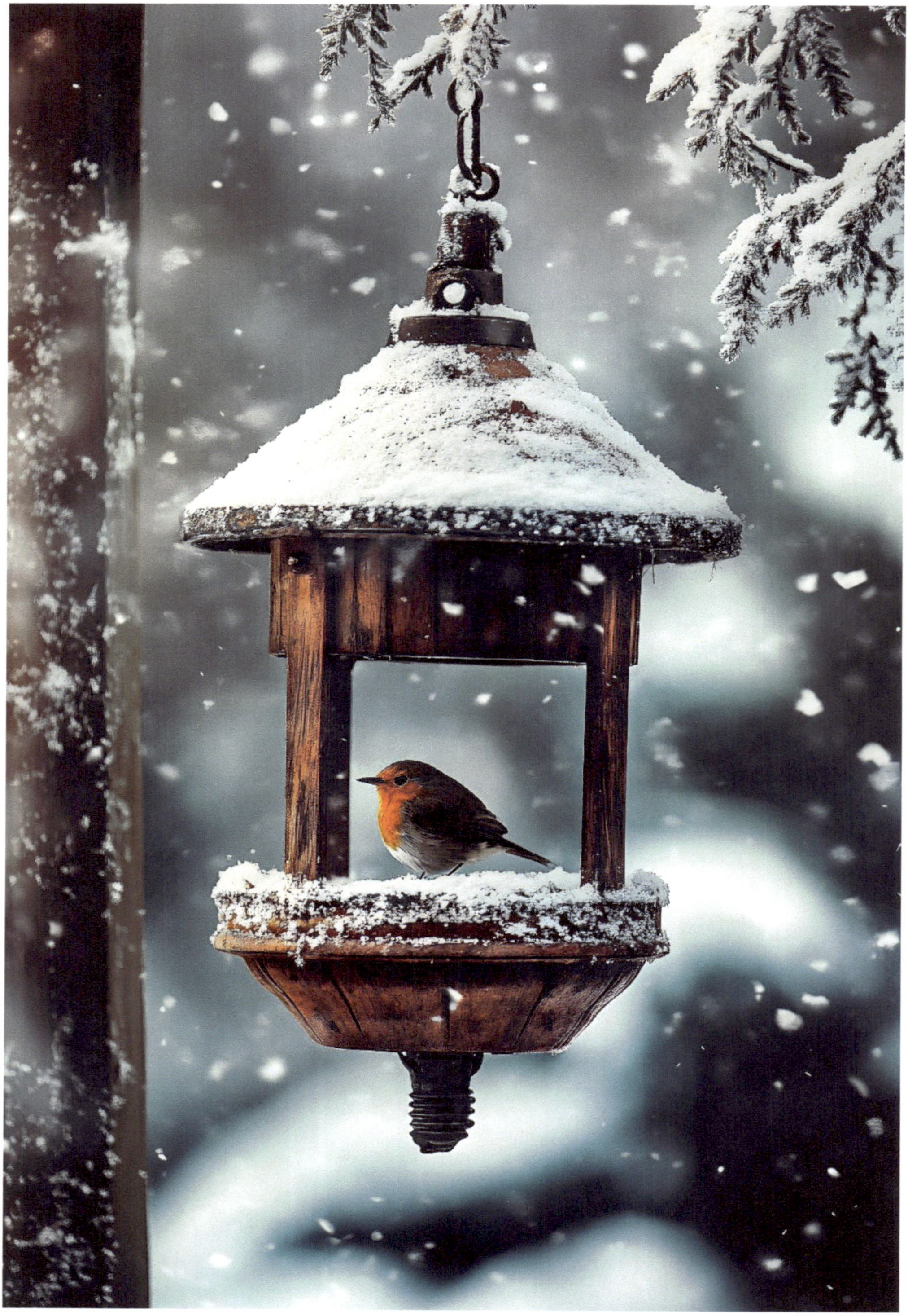

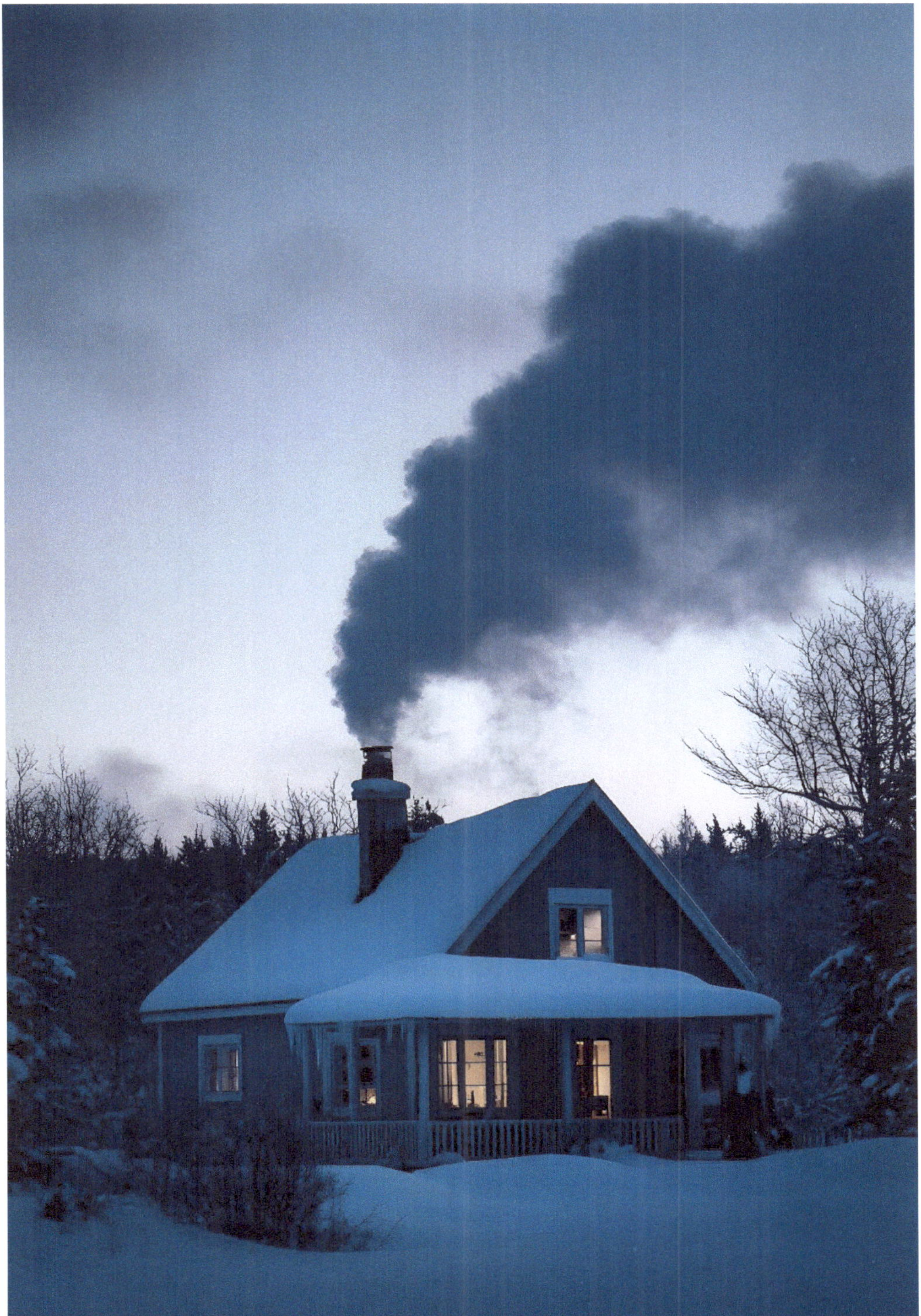

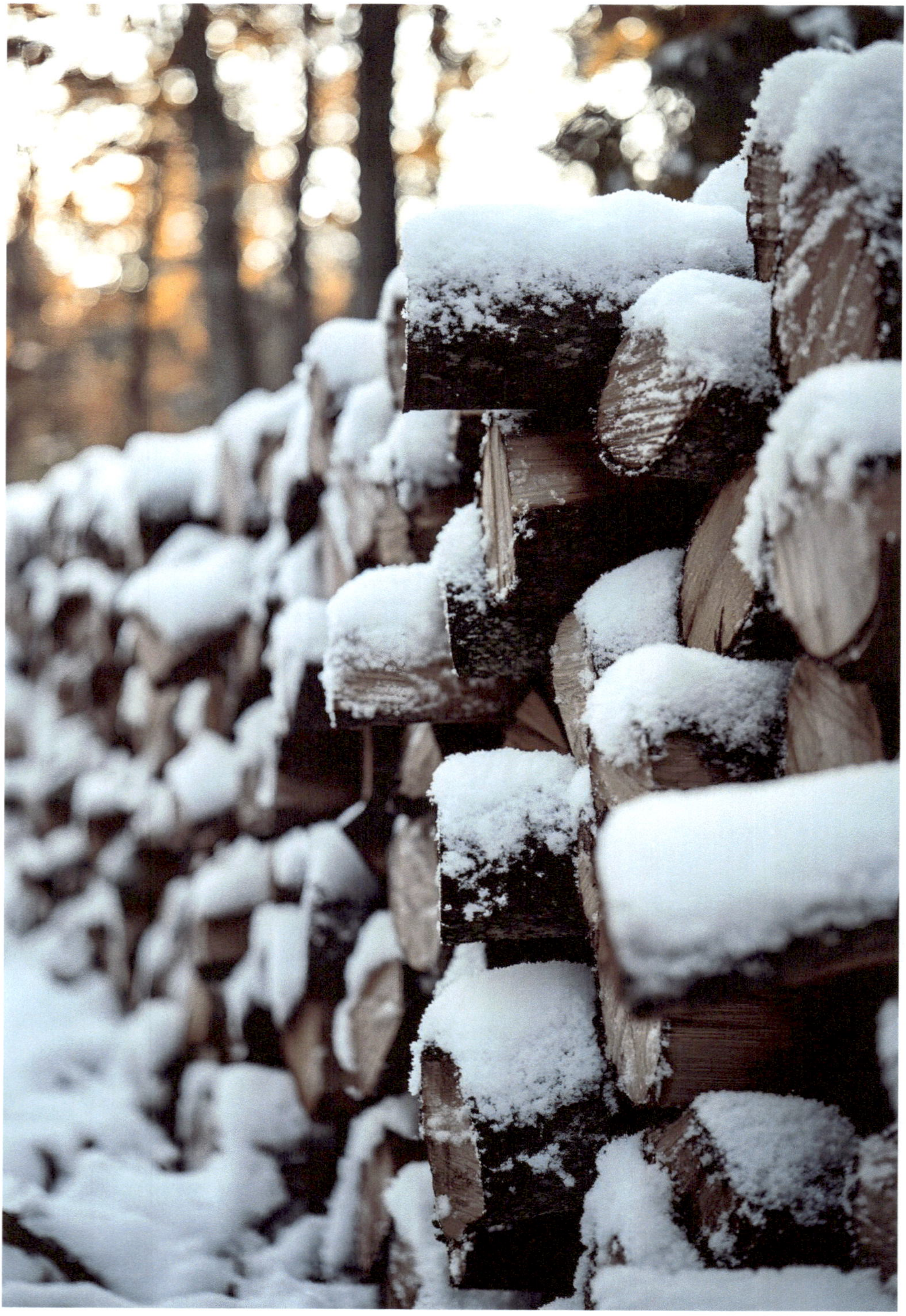

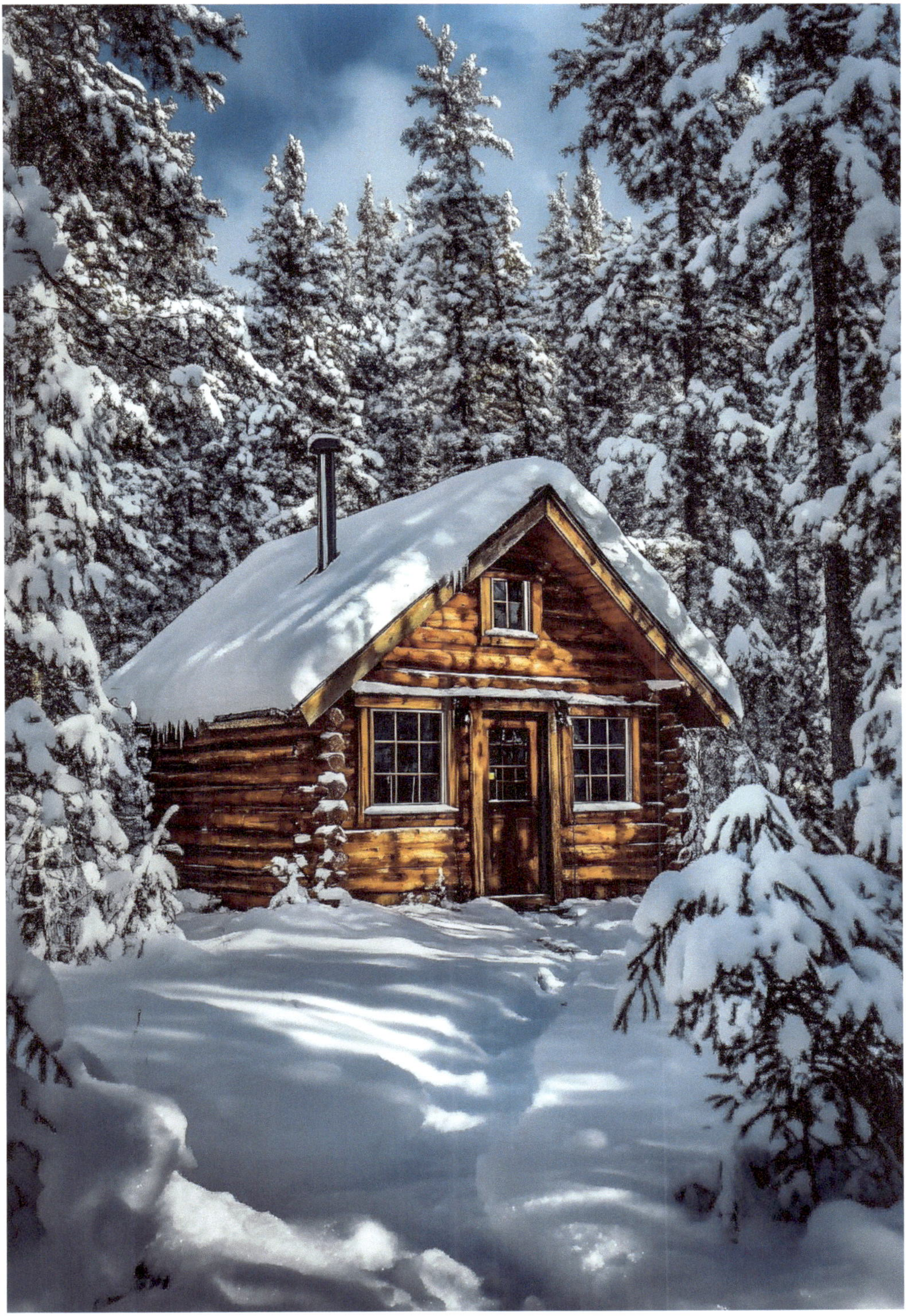

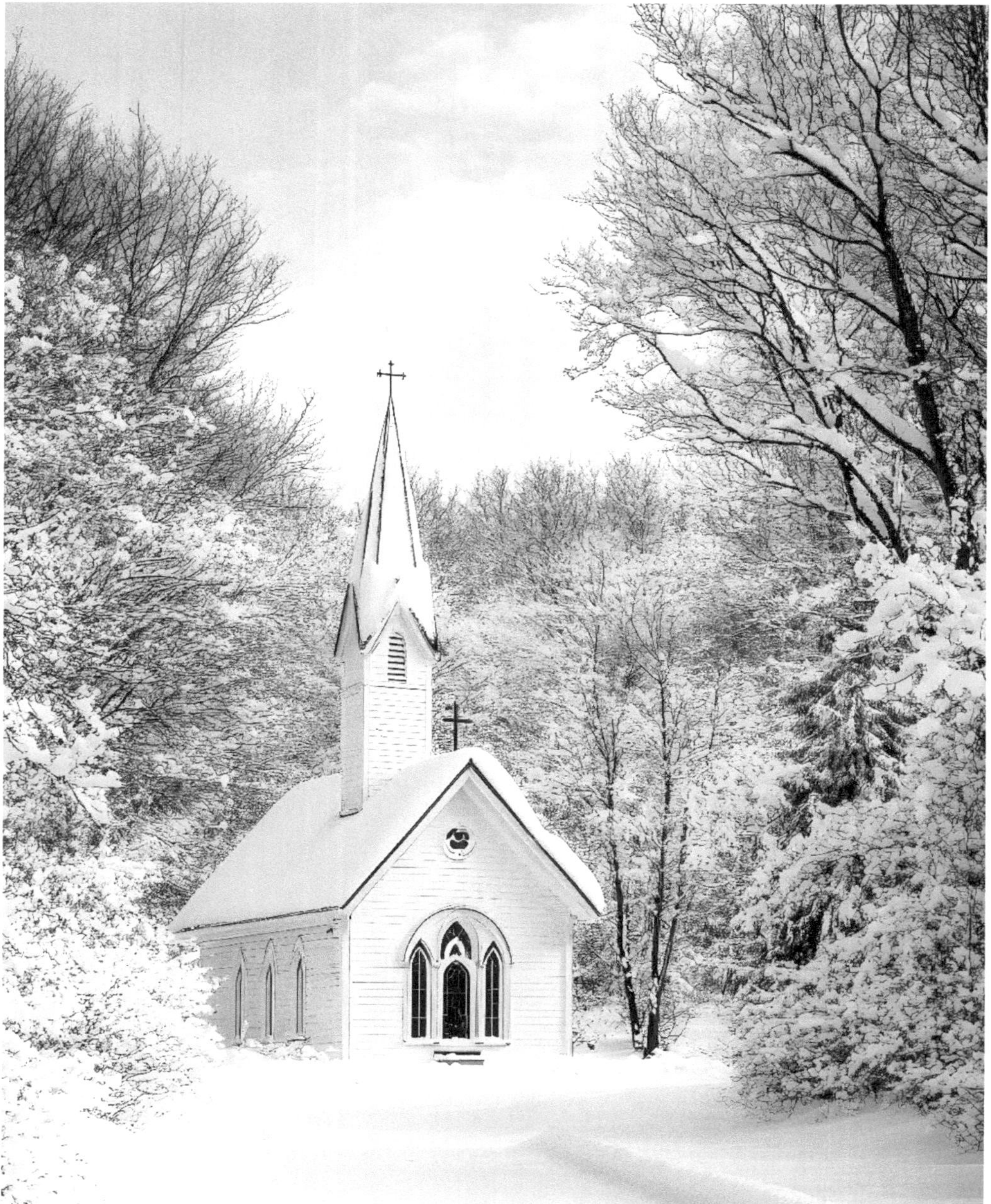

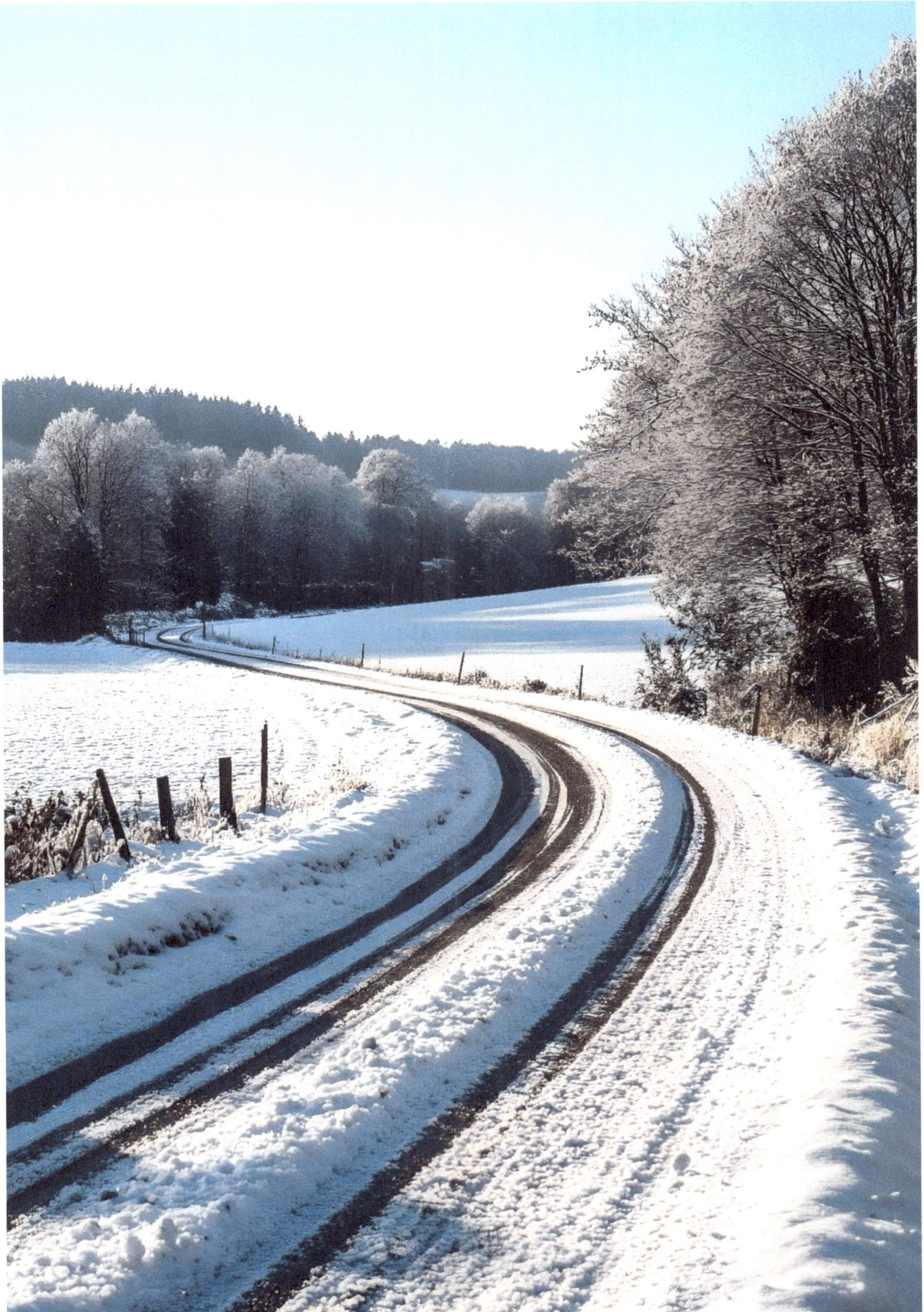

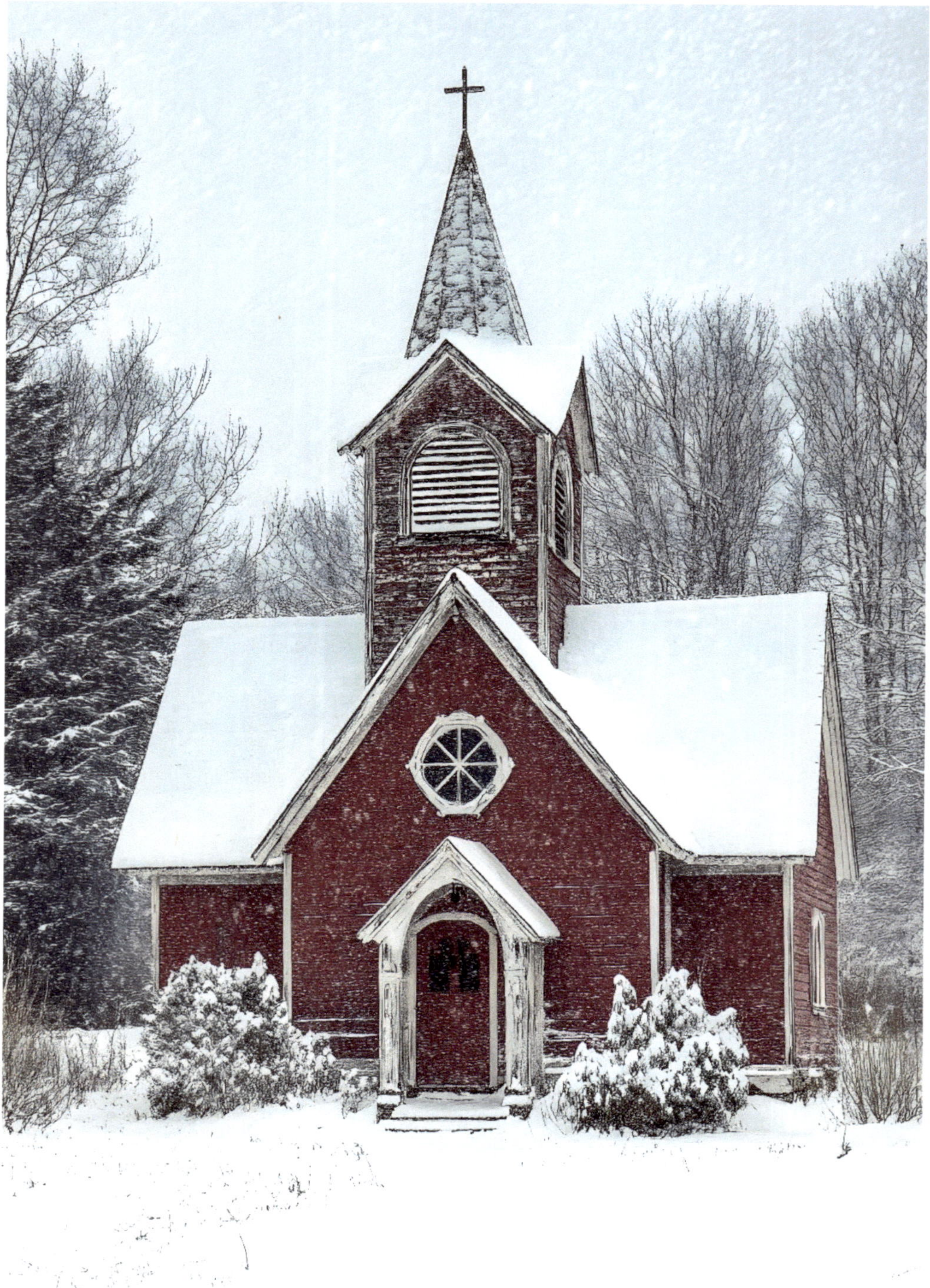

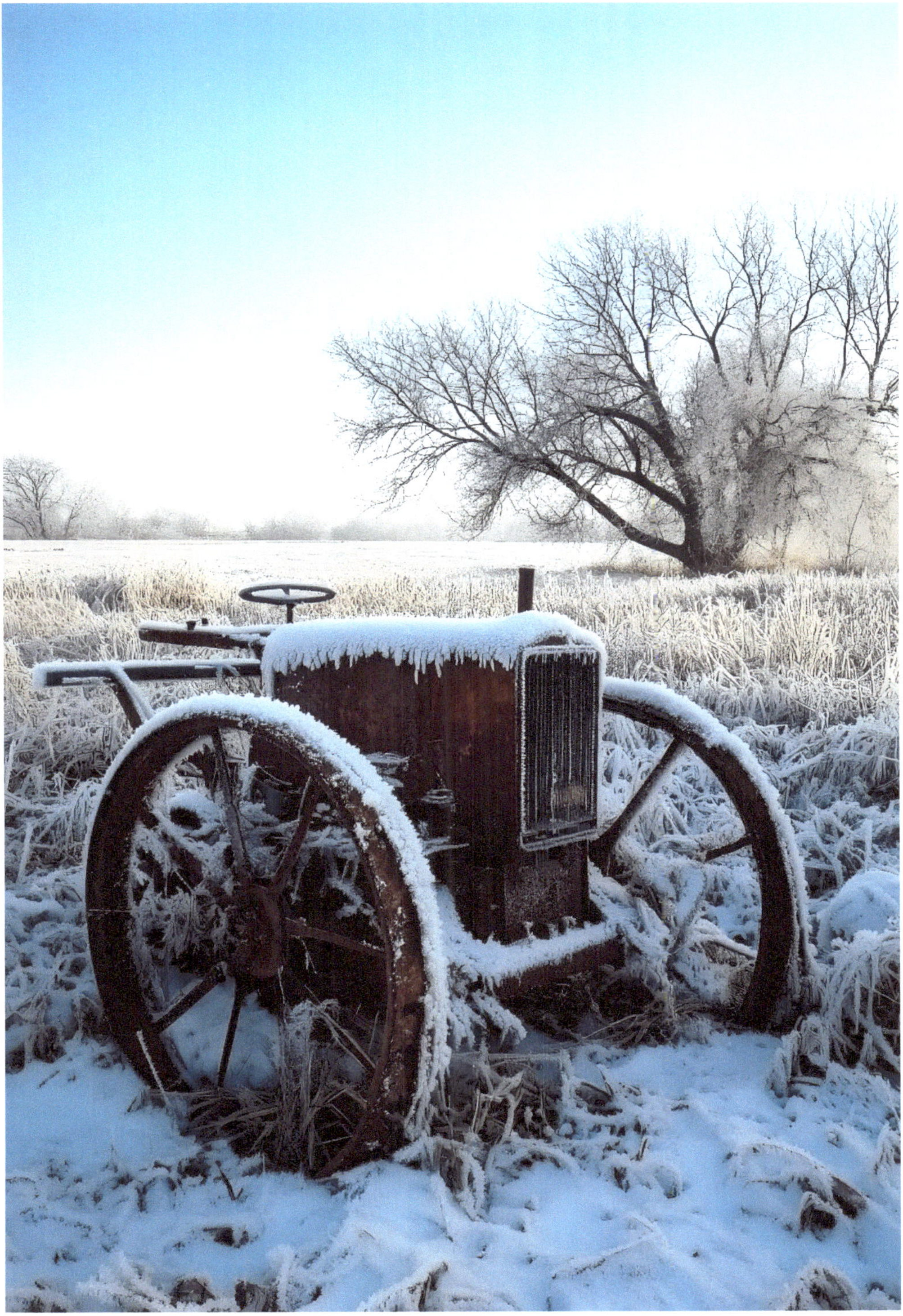

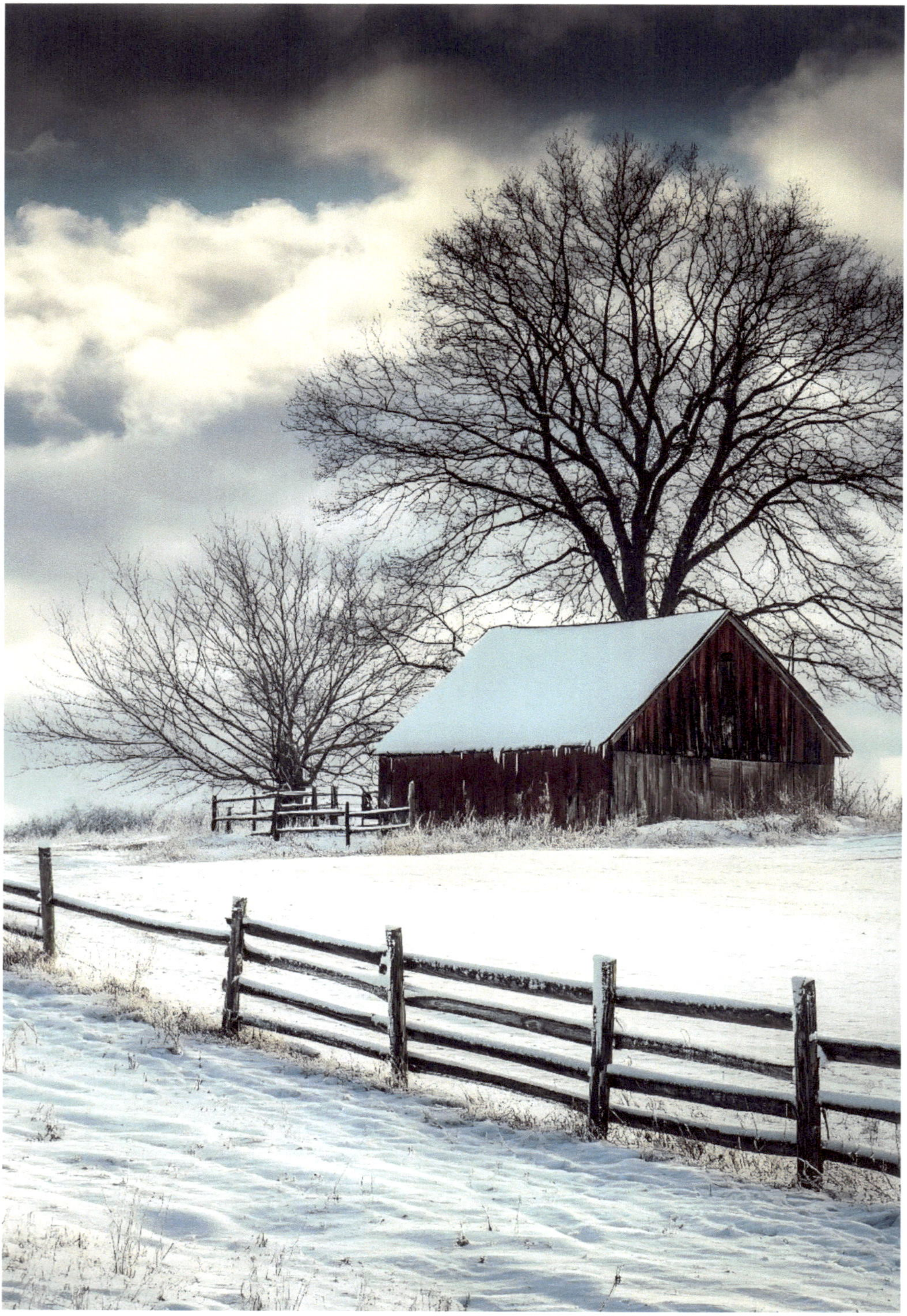

www.ingramcontent.com/pod-product-compliance
Lightning Source LLC
Chambersburg PA
CBHW040333220526
45473CB00009B/2671
* 9 7 9 8 3 3 6 6 9 1 5 3 5 *